NEWLY REVISED EDITION

Kabbalah Centre Publishing is a registered DBA of Kabbalah Centre International, Inc.

For further information:

The Kabbalah Centre
155 E. 48th St., New York, NY 10017
1062 S. Robertson Blvd., Los Angeles, CA 90035

1.800.Kabbalah
www.kabbalah.com

Printed in China, January 2026

Trade Paperback ISBN: 978-1-57189-996-5

Design: HL Design (Hyun Min Lee) www.hldesignco.com

www.kabbalah.com™

SATAN
AN AUTOBIOGRAPHY

FROM THE TEACHINGS OF
RAV BERG

TABLE OF CONTENTS

PART II:
THE TESTS

PART III: THE END OF RELIGION

PART IV: THE FINAL CHAPTER

1

PART I:

PITCHING THE PITCHFORK

CHAPTER ONE:
PLEASED TO MEET YOU

SYMPATHY FOR THE DEVIL

Satan writing an autobiography? Is this some kind of bad joke? Are you really trying to tell me this is a book of nonfiction?

OK, OK. I know you're suspicious, to say the least. And you have every right to be. After all, as a child, you may have read tales of people selling their souls to me, or, as a teenager, maybe you listened as the Rolling Stones described my role at crucial moments in history—tipping the scales toward crucifixion, the Holocaust, and all the unspeakable atrocities people perpetrate in my name.

More likely, you don't even believe that I exist. After all, anonymity and deception have been part of my strategy since the very beginning. Your disbelief certainly works for me. If nothing else, it's proof that I've been doing a good job.

But what if I were to tell you that whatever you think of me—or don't think of me—you're mistaken? Completely off the mark.

Just hear me out. The truth is that I'm very real, and very powerful, and you and I are locked in a deadly struggle. What's worse, I'm winning—that much I'm sure you'll acknowledge. Just take a look around. Under my influence, you've turned this world into one hell of a mess.

But here's what you don't know. Although I'm your Opponent in this Game of Life, *in the end, I'm just doing my job, and way down deep, I'm rooting for you to win.* I'll explain, but what you need to know right now is that you've been playing so badly that I've got to bend the rules to help you out.

I'm not who you think I am, and now is the time to set the record straight. Yes, I'm using this book to temporarily give up my most powerful weapon: Secrecy. When you don't believe I exist, or you misunderstand what I'm up to, I win hands down every time. But as it turns out, this isn't good for either one of us. Why? Because it screws up the plan God set in motion a long, long time ago.

Basically, you left the Garden of Eden. After that happened, God wanted to find a way for you to stop feeling so ashamed and to earn your way back. The way to overcome shame is to strive to stop acting selfishly, and to start giving—to be more like God. That's why God gave you free will; without using it to make good choices, you could never earn your way back to the Garden of Endless Light and fulfillment.

But if this assignment proved too easy for you, you wouldn't have truly earned anything. And that's where I came in. God gave me the job of providing you with obstacles to overcome; by resisting the temptations I put before you, you could bring more and more Light into this world, until finally everything would become Light, as it was in the beginning.

The problem is that I've done my job of opposing you a little too well, and you haven't done your job of resisting me well enough. As a result, we're falling behind schedule.

I know, I know. This is a lot for you to take in. So let's slow things down a bit.

WHY IT WORKS THIS WAY

People of every race can serve God on one condition: They have to believe. If you don't believe God exists, then how can you serve God?

That's one limitation I don't have. You do not have to believe in me in order to serve me!

Let that sink in for a moment. Now think about this: If you did believe in me—the real me—you would never, ever, serve me. Ironic, isn't it? That's why doubt is my very essence. It's not a philosophical statement. It's how I rule. Cynicism is my life force. Skepticism is the marrow of my being.

My power to rule over you thrives on disbelief.

Brilliant, isn't it?

You don't perceive me with your five senses. And it is your disbelief in me that gives me the power to influence this physical universe and control the hearts and minds of humankind.

If you saw the movie *The Usual Suspects*, you're familiar with the following line:

> *"The greatest trick the devil pulled was convincing the world he doesn't exist."*

Where do you think the line came from? Actually, I first slipped it into the mind of one Charles Baudelaire, the poet who lived in 19th century France. Baudelaire wrote:

> *"The devil's greatest deception is to convince us that he does not exist."*

Funny thing. Though Baudelaire channeled this profound statement into his writings, he did not believe in me. He said as much. And the paradoxical logic of his own statement troubled him deeply.

Does this surprise you?

THE POWER OF DISBELIEF

Of all the writers, poets, and philosophers that have written about me over the centuries, 99 percent of them got it wrong. Once in a while, I've let a few facts slip through the cracks to see if you would catch on.

Only a select few ever have.

French author and Nobel Prize winner, André Gide, had an inkling when he wrote this about me:

> *"He is never so well served as when he is unperceived."*

The old Frenchman also wrote:

> *"It's always to his interest not to let himself be recognized;*

and there, as I said, is what bothers me: to think that the less I believe in him, the more I strengthen him."

Dead on. I thrust skepticism into your rational mind to sustain my existence. I inject you with so much disbelief that it courses through your veins, floods your brain waves, and permits me to live unfettered behind a curtain of doubt.

And here's the kicker: To seal the deal, I make you believe these doubts are yours. Why? As long as you believe it's you, I remain invisible. As soon as you believe in me, it's Game Over. Get it? Doubt is not just a trick performed by "the devil," it is who I am.

IDENTITY CRISIS

All these years, I've let you think that you have ownership of the opinions and beliefs that arise in your mind. You are far more than your thoughts, but you hate giving up the idea that you're special—that those thoughts and ideas are uniquely your own. You don't distinguish between the two voices at work in your head (my voice and God's). You only hear my loud, limiting voice and all the negative thoughts that accompany my cacophony. And when you give in to my temptations, you think you've lost.

CAUSE AND EFFECT

I keep you focused completely on the effects, but never the true cause. Consider me the greatest special effects artist in history. You love watching all the special effects that I display in the movie that is your life. And that's exactly what your life is. It's a movie, with drama, suspense, fear, a few moments of comedy (when I am in a good mood), and lots and lots of tragedy.

Your life is what it is because you don't bother searching for the unseen source behind everything that transpires in your life ... or this world.

AT LONG LAST

The time has come to reveal my presence, to step out from behind the curtain and remove my mask. My real story has never been told. But I will tell it today. The need for putting God's plan back on track is urgent, and, with your help, that transformation gets jump-started right here. The pages that follow will make my true identity and purpose crystal clear.

Am I worried about revealing myself? You're kidding, right? The moment you close the book, the truth of who I am will begin to fade from your mind. But I'm hoping that even a glimpse of what's really going on can help restore things to their proper balance. It can give you the tools you need to play more effectively in this all-important Game we know as Life.

I cannot let you know me permanently. Never. I will not permit you to fully grasp the totality of who I am or the depth of my role in your universe. I'll plant the seed that this book is just a gimmick. An autobiography by Satan is just a creative device. Norman Mailer tried his hand at it. Others will follow. Nifty idea, but nothing that's going to rock my world.

Feel better now? Comfortable with your conclusions? Great, let's get on with my story.

WHAT'S IN A NAME

First, let's clear up a misconception about the word Satan. Check the history books. Satan is not my name. Surprised? Don't be. I'll explain. Is *pitcher* the name of Sandy Koufax? Is *love* the name of Mother Teresa? Is *center iceman* the name of Wayne Gretzky? Is *shooting guard* the name of Michael Jordan? Is *midfielder* the name of David Beckham? Is *industrialist* the name of Charles Michael Schwab? Is *singer* the name of Mariah Carey? Is *emperor* the name of Julius Caesar? No. These are not names. They're job descriptions. Same with *Satan*. It's not a name. It's a role I play in the Game of Life. Look in the Old Testament. Unravel an ancient Torah scroll. Inscribed on the parchment is the first-ever appearance of the word Satan in the history of literature. It's a Hebrew word. Translated accurately, *Satan* means "adversary." The Old Testament actually says "*HaSatan*," which means "the adversary," or "he who opposes."

In *Zechariah 3:1-2*, it reads:

> *1. Then he showed me Joshua the high priest standing before the Angel of the Lord, and* ***the Satan*** *standing at his right hand to oppose him. 2. And the Lord said to* ***the Satan****, "The Lord rebukes you,* ***the Satan****. The Lord who has chosen Jerusalem rebukes you! Is this not a brand plucked from the fire."*

When the Bible speaks of Satan, it's talking about an opposing power. Me. I am the antagonist in the movie of your life. I'll reveal the reason behind this in due time. Patience, my friend (never a strong point of yours, I must add).

The movie I speak of takes place in your head. That world around you is a mega IMAX screen, so to speak, and I am the only antagonist in the history of dramatic acting who is never seen or heard. I am invisible, even though I am everywhere. Such extraordinary magic! Such dazzling sleight of hand!

It's funny, because we think that in order to be an actor in the physical world you need a big ego. Well, I create the ego, yet, ironically, when I'm playing my role, no one sees me perform. Now if this is starting to sound very strange, relax. As we roll through history, it will all begin to make sense.

UNMASKING THE DEVIL

The most important thing I'd like you to realize at this stage is that there is no such thing as a devil. No such thing as a demon, at least not the way you think of it. So, who caused all this misconception? Why does the entire English-speaking world use an ancient Hebrew word (*Satan*) to inaccurately identify me? Why not just use the correct English translation and call me the Adversary?

CHAPTER TWO:
ONCE UPON A TIME IN THE UNIVERSE

THE BEGINNING OF EVERYTHING

This is my story. However, when I explain my origins you'll also learn something about your own. Let's first tackle Creation and the origins of this universe. Wouldn't you finally like to know where you really come from, and what you're doing here?

We're going to have to travel back—way, way back—to the beginning of it all. To the beginning of all beginnings. Long before Sir Isaac Newton and the Renaissance, before the Knights Templar in the Middle Ages, prior to the prophet Muhammad teaching in Mecca, before Jesus walked the Holy Land, before Siddhartha founded Buddhism, before Moses stood on Mount Sinai, and before Abraham discovered the unity underlying all reality—even before I seduced Adam and Eve in the Garden of Eden (I'll explain that episode later on). In fact, we've got to go back some 15 billion years ago and then roll back even more, just before the Big Bang and the notion of time popped into existence.

This is where the real story begins.

I could write volumes explaining the birth of the universe and the emergence of life on Earth. But I will dispense with all that. Real truth should be able to be reduced to a simple tale understood by all. What follows is the story of all stories, told in three short acts

Act I

Once upon a time, before the creation of the universe, there was an infinite Positive Force of Energy that you folks have the habit of calling God. This Energy filled all reality. There was nothing else besides this Energy, this Light.

Act II

One fine day, God decided to share all His Light, which consisted of love beyond love, bliss beyond bliss, and joy beyond joy. But there was no one with whom to share. So, God created a being to act as a recipient, to receive the goodness that God wanted to give. This being of receiving was one giant soul, which encompassed what would later become all the individual souls of humanity, even yours. This being was the Vessel.

Act III

God filled the Vessel with infinite happiness, whereupon both God and the Vessel lived happily ever after. Well, not quite...

A funny thing happened. For one brief moment during Act II—right before Happily Ever After was achieved—an extraordinary event occurred.

WHAT HAPPENED?

Not much, really. Only the development of the cosmos, including the entire history of human civilization up to and including the present moment, as well as all the events that will transpire tomorrow, leading up to the final destiny of the world!

From our perspective, that's a lot. But from the perspective of God, it transpired in less than a blink of an eye.

What follows is a concise account of what took place (and what is taking place right now). It is also the story of my life.

CHAPTER THREE:
THE MEANING OF LIFE

WHY DO WE NEVER GET AN
ANSWER WHEN WE'RE
KNOCKING AT THE DOOR?
WITH A THOUSAND MILLION
QUESTIONS ABOUT HATE
AND DEATH AND WAR.
—THE MOODY BLUES

THE QUESTION

I'll leave it to science to describe *how* physical creation happened. As for me, I will tell you *why* it happened, which is far more valuable. We start with the obvious question: If you were once soaking up infinite joy emanating directly from God, how did you end up here, today, in this fine mess? Where is God now? What happened to the infinite bliss? Where is the happy ending? Why did the Big Bang take place, giving birth to an airless, lightless, black vacuum?

Why did Happily Ever After give way to Miserably Ever More?

First, let me suggest that you should be raising these questions—not me! Therein lies one of your biggest problems. You don't ask enough tough questions. Instead, you watch TV. You eat. You gain weight, or obsess about staying thin. You complain. You read tabloids. You're fixated on celebrities, making idols of people that are every bit as lost and confused as you are, and probably more so.

You do as little as you can get away with. You wait around for things to change, or for someone to bail you out. But no one does because they are in the same boat.

You seek fulfillment from outside sources and get-rich-quick schemes. Or you work 70 hours a week to avoid facing reality—and your family. You worship money instead of searching for the truth. And all the while, you turn a blind eye to the suffering of others and a deaf ear to the cries of humanity.

Victimhood is the flag you fly. You believe that the universe has dealt you a lousy hand. You're convinced life is random, grossly unfair, and coldly indifferent to your pain and suffering. It's a dog-eat-dog existence, so you don't have the time to think about it, much less question it; you've got to get as much as you can for yourself. Or, you just don't plain give a crap about anything. At all.

Those of you who do ask questions only ask *how.* You never ask *why.* When you ask *how,* you are dealing with the symptom. It's only when you ask why that you are addressing the real cause.

Big difference. Really big difference.

Well, it's time to wake up! Start asking real questions. And don't stop there. Start demanding real answers, too! Try your hand at a few meaningful conversations while you're at it, and see how you feel.

I am going to lay it on the line here, so you won't have any more excuses. I'm writing this book so you can lift the level of your game. In this manuscript, I spill my secrets. The tough questions will be raised and answered. And we're going to engage in meaningful conversation as it relates to the story of my life—and, more importantly, your life. So let's begin with you. Let's find out what it is you are doing here on this small blue planet floating in a galaxy that appears to be spinning precisely in the middle of nowhere.

JONI MITCHELL AND THE MEANING OF LIFE

Joni Mitchell got it right. She nailed it with one line of lyrics from her song, *Big Yellow Taxi*, a major hit back in the 1960s. Incidentally, you gave me a run for my money during this turbulent decade. Love. Peace. Freedom. Flower power. You got close. But by the time the seventies rolled on by, I had managed to regain a foothold. By the eighties, I had turned that foothold into a stranglehold. I flipped "Make love, not war" into "Greed is good." In the nineties, I started putting you to sleep with a choke hold.

By the turn of the millennium, you were out. All that was left inside your head was a pilot light. That remaining flicker of consciousness could only produce a fixation on paparazzi, celebrity, microchips, and digital toys, leaving you blind to anything of substance and meaning. Even your so-called spirituality was shallow. It was always about temporary relief, never long-term solutions. It was about idolizing so-called gurus instead of enriching the lives of people.

So are politicians. And religious authorities. And the whole crowd in Silicon Valley, top to bottom. Scholars are a slam dunk. Physicists, a cakewalk. Wall Street bean counters, a home run. You'd fall off your chair if you knew how easy it is to manipulate all these folks.

Anyway, your false spirituality, your smugness, your pride, and your greed keep you from discovering the underlying cause of your problems. But I've got some good news for you. I'm going to help you do that now.

Let's return to that Joni Mitchell lyric:

> *"Don't it always seem to go, you don't know what you got 'til it's gone; they paved paradise and put up a parking lot."*

There it is. Right in front of you. In black and white. A lyric that captures the essence of all Scripture.

What's the secret within the lyric?

CREATING CONSCIOUSNESS

When you—humanity, the One Soul—were originally created, you had it all. Everything. Unimaginable happiness. Unfathomable pleasure. Inconceivable fulfillment. But there was no appreciation. No genuine joy in the depth of your being. No awareness of what you truly had. Talk about taking something for granted! Let me explain.

Are you happy you don't have a migraine headache right now? Of course you are. Were you aware of this happiness three seconds ago? Do you know why you weren't? Your desire for this happiness was already fulfilled; therefore, you were oblivious to it. Get it? If a pounding, nauseating pain should start filling your skull, you'd become aware of this desire pretty fast.

Now, what happens when you have a migraine and the pain finally subsides? Suddenly you're the happiest and most appreciative person on the planet. Your desire has been fulfilled, and you're definitely feeling good about it. You now appreciate your pain-free existence!

Don't it always seem to go, you don't know what you got 'til it's gone...

In Act I of our Creation story, God created the human soul. The soul possessed infinite desires, and God filled every one of those desires with every conceivable form of happiness and pleasure imaginable. But the soul was oblivious. Unconscious. Why? The soul had been created in a perfect state of total fulfillment, right from the very first moment.

Are you following this? Just the way you were unconscious, unappreciative, of your migraine-free existence a second ago, the soul was unconscious and unappreciative of its perfect existence. The soul had no grasp of all that it was receiving. Why? The soul knew nothing else. It was made that way.

Genuine happiness can only be understood and appreciated when contrasted against the absence of happiness—unhappiness. If I am going to tell you all about myself for the first time in history, you need to understand this Universal Law. This is the way seedlings of consciousness are created.

The soul could only come to know and appreciate God by experiencing the absence of God and the loss of the fulfillment it once knew. Once the soul experienced the absence of God, only then could it be aware of the presence of God.

REPERCUSSIONS

The implications of this Law are disturbing when you stop and think about it. So, take a minute. Right now. Think. Real hard. I'll stop inserting myself for this one moment and allow you some clarity.

The clock is ticking. Start reading...

You only value something by its absence. Candlelight is worthless on a sunlit day, yet it's precious in the dark of night. You can recognize fulfillment only after having experienced emptiness.

I'm back.

As I said, the implications of this truth are frightening. How so? Well, in the beginning your soul was created full of contentment. That was all you knew. You were unaware of what you really had. You felt not one ounce of appreciation or consciousness.

Sit down. Take a breath. Now, brace yourself.

If the soul initially receives unimaginable happiness and it's suddenly taken away, what's left? Unimaginable sadness and depression!

If the soul was swimming in a sea of blissful pleasure, what remained when that sea disappeared? A desert of unbearable pain!

If the soul enjoyed indescribable serenity and it was removed in an instant, what was left? Indescribable chaos!

If God and truth are removed from the soul's existence, what remains? Nothing but a Godless reality of lies and superstitions.

And, finally, the big one: If the soul was in a luminous dimension of immortality, which suddenly vanishes, what's left? The dark dimension of death! And that's what happened. The soul had no choice but to enter an opposite reality: One that includes pain, sadness, chaos, corruption, and deep depression. This is right around the time that the Big Bang occurred, and the physical universe burst into existence.

THE FIRST EFFECT

I'll let you in on another secret. The Big Bang was my first special effect. I don't just mean the spectacular explosion; I mean it was an actual Effect—as in, it was the result of a previous Cause.

This is a Cause that your entire world has no knowledge of, and I will divulge it in due time.

With the Big Bang, a process of learning for all of humanity was set into motion. Along this steep curve lie the purpose of this world and the meaning of life: To create a dimension where you can truly appreciate and forever enjoy the endless goodness that is your birthright. Unfortunately, based on the Universal Law you've just learned, your ego needs to experience pain and loss in order for you to appreciate this endless goodness. There's always a catch, isn't there?

CHAPTER FOUR:
SATAN'S GIG

PAIN

This is all insanity. How can any human being possibly endure the nightmarish, hellish, diabolical dimension we find ourselves in? But you know what? You've been doing just that. For millennia, you've been imprisoned by unspeakable suffering. But how can this be if God is supposed to be all-powerful? Why wouldn't God do something about this? After all, isn't God the worker of miracles? God can conjure up solutions to any problems, right? Absolutely correct. There is nothing God cannot do.

And God came up with a solution to this little dilemma, too. In fact, God never planned to sit back and watch you suffer. God is compassionate. Merciful. God's all about unconditional love. So, God thought about the situation, and came up with a way for you to experience the absence of God without having to endure unending pain.

That's one hell of a paradox: How can one truly comprehend pain, chaos, sadness, depression, and death without experiencing pain, chaos, sadness, depression, and death? Luckily for you, in the Realm of the Infinite, all paradoxes are resolved. God solved the problem, and did it by putting me to good use.

Now, it's starting to get interesting...

So what about this business of *feeling* pain and loss without actually having to *experience* the pain and loss? Sounds like a magician's trick, doesn't it? But God found a way to help you circumvent the very system you (the Vessel) asked for. When you wanted to receive, but also be like God, you were basically saying to God, "Stay out of my life, but rescue me if the going gets rough."

So, that is exactly what God did. God arranged it so that you:

- Could feel the potential pain, but not have to go through the actual pain.
- Could let your stunt double, your ego, take the hit instead of having to take the hit yourself.
- Could choose proactive short-term pain instead of long-term suffering.
- Could have a constant awareness of pain and its purpose.

Now, let's break each one of God's solutions down a little further.

FEELING THE POTENTIAL PAIN

You can choose to feel potential pain, so you don't have to experience the real thing. At any given moment, you can lose it all, or rather, I can take it all away: Your loved ones, your security, your position, your children, your health, your well-being, your future. That constant awareness helps you to care for, enjoy, and be fulfilled in every moment of life. This is the easiest way to avoid pain. It is also the reason why I have kept myself concealed for so long. Once you know my game, you can just play it without me! And what would be the fun in that for me?

Imagine betrayal by your spouse, or a sudden loss of health or money, or a threat to the safety or well-being of your children. Make it so real you can taste it. Take a good look at your life and start appreciating everything you have taken for granted, because, otherwise, I own you. One tsunami, one Twin Towers, one collapsed financial institution, one disease, one child predator, and I've got your life in my hands.

The lesson here? It's simple. Love your mate with greater intensity, take care of your health with greater intention, work at your job with greater care, and be present for your children with greater joy. See the paradise that surrounds you, so I don't replace it with a parking lot! Get it? Appreciation and gratitude are powerful antidotes to pain, and God gave them to you expressly for this purpose. You've been holding the cure all the time, and you just didn't realize it.

THE STUNT DOUBLE, THE EGO

God didn't stop there. He gave you yet another cure, another tool, another antidote to your suffering. And it comes in the form of Harrison Ford. OK, not quite, but I wanted to make sure I had your undivided attention.

You see, Harrison Ford is a handsome movie star. When he played the role of Indiana Jones, you can bet your bottom dollar the movie studio didn't want to see its star actor performing all those dangerous stunts.

Enter the stunt double.

The stunt double is a highly trained, extremely skilled stuntman who assumes all the risk of pain and injury on behalf of the movie star. That's his job, and he gets paid well to do it. All Harrison Ford has to do is step aside and allow the stunt double to take his place in a potentially dangerous scene.

God devised a similar solution for the movie that is your life. God created a stunt double to take on all the pain on your behalf. All humankind had to do was step aside every time a potentially dangerous or uncomfortable situation arose, and allow the stunt double to do his thing. But humankind never did. You don't, either. Nor do your friends. No one does.

How do I know this? Because....

I AM THE STUNT DOUBLE!

I know. Hard to believe, right? You thought I was the source of all evil. The Prince of Darkness. Father of Lies and Deceit. The Tempter. The Son of Perdition.

You thought I was here to ruin your life, to darken human existence, and to destroy the world. Hardly. I was given my job to act as your official stand-in by God. I am here to help you. Surprise!

Now, if the term *stunt double* sounds too Hollywood for you, you can just call me your ego. Yes, that's right. I am your ego. My vocation is an essential part of God's plan. Like I said earlier, the soul came to the parking lot to experience pain in order to awaken appreciation for the paradise that is God. And there are two ways to experience pain:

1. *You* experience it.
2. Or *I* do.

I'll be more specific. There are two ways to know the pain of this world:

1. Through the decimation of your ego and all self-interest.
2. Through pain inflicted on your body and soul.

Life throws you a curveball. You either allow me, the ego, to become frustrated and worried. Or *you* will.

Life throws you a sinker ball. The ego gets depressed. Or *you* will.

In other words, all kinds of garbage will hit you throughout your life. You either let the ego be sad, depressed, ashamed, or hurt, or *you* will experience sadness, depression, madness, aggravation, and a whole lot of hurt (great lyrics for a country song, I might add).

After a lifetime of living with your fellow man, either the ego dies—or you die. Catch that last one? I slipped it in without much fanfare. Here it is again: Death occurs for one reason—you fail to let the ego die. Everyone throughout history has died as a result of protecting their ego. They hang on to it for dear life. But if the ego itself dies, you live forever. Really. Truly. If humankind wiped ego from the face of the Earth, it would be the end of all death! Earth would be transformed into an endless spiritual and physical paradise.

So, it's even my job to die for you—if you'd only let me. But you don't. You wind up experiencing all the pain. You do all the dying, while I do all the living. I've been hanging out on this Earth, living large for countless centuries while you all have been dropping like flies.

So why on Earth would you refuse to stand aside if unimaginable happiness and immortality are waiting for you? The answer is simple: Because you didn't know you had a stunt double. You simply weren't aware that my services were available. Well, now you know.

But before we move on, you might still be confused about this notion of ego. After all, I have spent millennia attempting to distort its true meaning. Your ego is your reactive response to the world.

For instance:

- You react to failure and get depressed. That is your ego.
- You respond to success and develop a swelled head. That's ego, too.
- You react to an opportunity and feel you're not good enough to seize it. Believe it or not, that is ego also.
- You seize an opportunity, pushing everyone else aside without regard for the pain you cause them. Ego strikes again.
- You are selfish. Ego.
- You give charity and let everyone know about it. Ego.
- Someone takes up a belief that is contrary to yours and you lock horns. Ego on both sides.
- Someone espouses an argument or belief that you agree with and you follow along blindly. Ego, ego, ego.

I do hope you're catching on. The ego's job is to motivate you to react. Everything you do at the ego's request in life is a knee-jerk reaction. I don't care what the trigger is, or what your intention is. Your ego sees to it that you're always reacting to someone or something. And I am the one inciting your behavior.

That means that all of the negative thoughts in your head are mine. However, because I've disguised myself so ingeniously in your ego, you think those thoughts are yours. And therein lies your problem.

Who do you think talks you out of dieting when the authentic you makes a commitment to lose weight? It's not the chocolate cake that makes you succumb. It's me, yours truly! I crank up your desire while simultaneously decreasing your willpower. It's a potent one-two punch. Then, I rationalize your defeat by whispering, "Don't worry, you can start again on Monday."

And sabotaging diets is only the tip of my iceberg!

PROACTIVE PAIN VERSUS SUFFERING

Fortunately for you, God gave you a custom-designed tool for overcoming ego—your ability to choose proactive, short-term pain instead of being bridled with lifelong misery. But I compromise you day in and day out. I convince you that it is better to "keep the peace" than to speak the truth. Sure, there is a way to really keep the peace, but it is not by keeping your mouth shut when something needs to be said. It is not about being nice when difficult actions must be taken. It is not about coping; it's about dealing.

God doesn't want you to merely cope. Sure, you can absorb a lot of pain, but you are not supposed to. You are meant to take on the momentary discomfort of confronting that difficult situation, but instead you push aside the truth and become full of pride and self-righteousness. You are supposed to *earn* paradise. Do you think you are going to do that by playing Mr. Nice Guy? That's one of my favorites: The person who thinks he is so brave when, in truth, he is a coward. He might be nice to your face, but, behind your back, he'll throw you under the bus to protect his good name.

Just stand up and deal with the difficult situation in front of you! Why do you think it's there? So you can sweep it under the rug? Face it: It is your challenger, it is your opposition, it is your adversary. So, get in the ring and fight. If you keep hiding, I win.

That's because when you live with pain, over time you become bitter. You come to believe that the world and God are out to get you. Admit it. You're never happy. OK, sometimes you feel that you are "good." But being good doesn't help you reach the potential you came to this world to achieve. You can try to justify your position by convincing yourself that righteous people like yourself are always tested. But deep inside, you live with the knowledge that you could be so much more. But you haven't got the strength to make that happen. I've taken it all away.

If you keep going the way you are going, I will have to send you something more difficult to deal with until you finally wake up—until you finally realize that confronting your difficulties is not nearly as painful as the suffering you are enduring now. So, do yourself a favor. Look at the situation. See me in it, fight me, and win. The pain you feel will dissolve and you will re-earn your place in the Garden.

CONSTANT AWARENESS

Even if you fail over and over again to activate any of God's solutions to the pain problem, God still leaves the window open for you. Even if you're living with the most incredible pain there is—physical suffering, the loss of a child, a barren existence, an empty stomach and pocketbook, a no-way-out sign—there is still a door to paradise.

If I have won every battle up until this point, if you have taken your life for granted, if you have been an egomaniac, if you have been a righteous coward, if you are truly suffering, then the only way to win at this late stage is to recognize that it's a game. Remember the goal is paradise. God did not forget you; you just haven't been playing very well.

So, how do you get back in the Game from here? You recognize the game you're in and you keep playing. The pain will not last forever. If the end goal is Eden, then there must be a bigger picture that you don't see. Start putting God's solutions to work. Start to appreciate this moment, and stop feeling like a victim. Let the ego do its job. Sure, you think you look bad; you lost what seems like everything; you feel humiliated by your wife, by your circumstances, by your physical condition. Great! The more humiliated the ego is, the better off you are. Be happy that I am getting hit. The more I get hit, the faster I get hurt, the more paradise you will earn back. Act unselfishly for a change. Help someone who is worse off than you. That's the straight path to paradise. Instead of letting me dance while you suffer, it's time to turn the tables.

YOU THINK YOU'RE TOUGH

I play hard, which means you get my very best every time out. It has to be this way. If it were easy for you—if it took no effort on your part—to find me and defeat me, you'd earn nothing. And nothing would have changed since you lost paradise. You need to earn your way back because that is the only way you can appreciate the infinite happiness that is your destiny. There's no way around it. That's why I have to use every trick in the book, every means possible, to make it difficult for you to find me. And, remember, I do this for your own good; without me, you won't have an Opponent in the game, which means winning would be meaningless.

I serve a noble cause, and the stakes are high. Your eternal happiness is on the line. So, to make sure you earn your bliss and evolve the level of consciousness and appreciation that will allow you to savor paradise for all time, I must be prepared to play tough.

Make no mistake, I can do that. *I am ruthless.* I have watched you fall on battlefields; waste away from cancer; suffer paralysis from stroke; bury your children; get robbed, raped, and molested by monsters; and experience every other hideous form of suffering. I couldn't hold back. I am under oath to use any and every means possible to deceive and conquer you.

You are the one who asked to make this process challenging so that you could enjoy the full measure of happiness that rightfully belongs to you. This path could have been easier. But if you don't allow the ego to experience 100 percent of the pain, you will never experience 100 percent of the pleasure. You wanted it all. You asked for it all. You are the one who empowered me to give you my very best.

THE REAL PAIN-INDUCER

Would you like to know a shortcut to kicking the pain habit? Simple. Renounce selfishness. Selfishness is a tool specifically designed to inflict repeated pain upon yourself. Sure, when you renounce selfishness, it'll hurt like hell—but that fleeting pain is the only pain you'll have to experience. There's your magic formula. Yep, that's the ticket. Give selfishness the boot and say *hello* to eternal life.

This is a good time for me to mention that I, myself, am the epitome of selfishness. In fact, *selfishness* would be my middle name if I had one. My job is to incite within you selfish behavior in all its manifestations: Egocentricity. Self-indulgence. Self-centeredness. Low self-esteem. Depression. Anger. Jealousy. Worry. Fear. Believe it or not, these are all different expressions of selfishness. Your task is to reject it. Overcome it. Resist it. My job is to convince you to embrace it with open arms.

But in spite of that—in spite of me—you have to suck it up. Yes, that's right. I'm telling you to get over it. Because if you can, this pain will be all that you need to endure during your life to earn the everlasting happiness that was originally given to you in Act I of our Creation Story.

THE TWO FOLD PROBLEM

Here's the two fold problem of humanity:

1. You've been living selfishly, under my control, for countless centuries. This is why the world bleeds.
2. You don't believe I exist. That is why the world continues to hemorrhage and suffer, ignorant of the way out.

The trouble begins in your head. Your consciousness. Actually, it's my consciousness inside your head. Every problem on Earth—from poverty, global warming, and disease to child pornography and substance abuse—is rooted in the collective, egocentric, selfish behavior of your fellow man.

These external problems in the world are symptoms. Not the Cause. Even if you fix global warming by reducing carbon emissions, the negativity from your selfish behavior will create another global problem. If you drive with road rage—even if you are driving a "green car"—your negativity will still cause lethal damage. You guys call it the butterfly effect. No way! It is *my* effect.

Consider this: What if ego was the cause of some exotic virus that threatened to kill millions of people? Then what you'd need is a miracle. What is a miracle? Think about it—it is an event that takes place outside the laws of physical nature. You make miracles happen when you overcome the laws of your ego nature. When you put the needs of another before your own selfish agenda, a miracle cure will show up on the planet as a reflection of the change that took place inside you.

Of course, my job right now is to make you say, "Baloney!" And it's working, isn't it? You're still skeptical!

This is precisely how I prevent you from achieving miracles.

TAKING OWNERSHIP

As you begin to renounce selfishness and overcome ego, gradually you come to the realization that the ego is not you. Not an easy task. But when you do get there, you're happy that I am the one going through hell and not you. When you reach a level of wisdom—let's call it a state of awareness—where you genuinely understand that it is me behind your ego, you'll be excited to put an end to the Game. For good.

But it takes a lifetime—typically many lifetimes—to achieve that elevated state of consciousness. Over the centuries, I've watched tough men weep, run like sissies, shake in their boots, soil themselves, commit suicide, and literally die of a heart attack when faced with a bruised ego. That is to say, it takes nothing less than Herculean effort to willingly allow the ego to experience pain so that your body and soul can choose happiness.

The reason a grown man fears the death of his ego more than he fears physical death is because he mistakes the ego for himself. He doesn't know it's me, his real enemy. He doesn't know that if the ego dies, he lives.

Be honest with yourself. If you actually knew—right now— that I was real, that I was the Cause of all your pain, you'd send me packing. This is why I work so hard to convince you I don't exist. If you really knew the truth, you'd welcome humiliation. You'd keep your big mouth shut when that arrogant, swaggering loudmouth friend of yours runs his mouth off. You'd stop yourself from one-upping him because you'd know it was me—inside of you—who was really pushing your buttons.

The thought of surrendering the ego is terrifying! But the fearsome threat is just a mirage. It is I who conjure up the fear, injecting it into every cell in your body. Thanks to me, facing this fear can seem almost impossible. But it isn't. Not only is it entirely possible, but overcoming your fear and squaring off against your ego is a very smart play. A winning move, without question.

But if you choose the alternative route of protecting the ego, you will suffer instead. Sickness. Disease. Emotional turmoil. Financial instability. Wrecked marriages. Ruined relationships. Chronic depression. Death. You know the routine. You know it well. All too well.

As long as you fail to make the separation between the real you and the real me, you will wind up taking on every ounce of pain throughout your entire life. This is the way it's been since the dawn of human consciousness.
Now you have it—my complete Game Plan.

I'm busted.

JOB

I am sure you all know the story of Job. If you don't know the story, and even if you do, it's time to hear it from my point of view, so listen up.

Job lived in the land east of Palestine a very long time ago. He was considered a righteous man, and you know how I love to undermine the righteous. So, I disguised myself as God and I rewarded him for his "piety" with great wealth, thousands of head of livestock, and a large family. In my book, this was a man with one hell of an ego who needed to be taught a lesson. I knew if I could push his buttons just so, I could break him down. That was my plan, anyway.

I went to God and challenged him to test Job. I wagered that if God started messing around with Job's family and possessions, Job would curse God. But God wouldn't do it, so I had to do my own dirty work. One day, robbers came and drove away all Job's cattle and slew his servants, and a terrible tornado from the desert destroyed the house in which Job's children were gathered. It killed them all. Much to my disbelief, not only did Job not curse God, he actually praised God. I was stunned, I have to tell you. This Job character was making me look bad. But I wasn't through with him yet.

I went back and tried to convince God that if Job were to be stricken by disease, then he might show his true colors. Again, I was reminded that God doesn't work that way. So, I worked my own magic and Job was stricken with the most terrible disease imaginable—leprosy. Even his wife began to persuade him to complain against God! Gotta love her! His friends joined in the complaining.

But—would you believe it?—Job remained firm and didn't curse God for a second. He praised God, and even called God his Redeemer. The guy was afflicted with a terrible skin disease and he still saw God's beauty. Talk about keeping the faith and never losing sight of the bigger picture! Job used the very tools that I told you about just a few pages ago—a man well ahead of his time. Admittedly, had I known that he would be such a tough nut to crack, I would have wagered on someone else, that's for sure.

But how would anyone have known had I not done my job and tested the waters? Note the connection between the name *Job* and my doing my *job*. The Bible is code, you know. These nice little stories contain more layers of meaning than you could uncover in a lifetime of study. And I am just beginning to scratch the surface. You might be wondering how the story ended. It probably comes as no surprise—if you know the true nature of God—that Job was rewarded, handsomely. He regained his health and wealth, his family grew, and he lived another 140 years.

The story of Job should open your eyes to the fact that absolutely no one is immune from playing the pain game. Not the good, not the pious, not the righteous. Everyone will encounter pain, but it's also true that anyone can choose to turn that pain into abundance and happiness. You just have to be willing to take the initial hit, swallow your pride, and turn this tiresome, self-imposed game around.

CHAPTER FIVE:
FIGHTING BACK!

BEATING ME AT MY OWN GAME

Besides letting me take the pain for you, which ultimately weakens my power over you, the next best way to beat me is to starve me. I begin to waste away the moment you become a conscious being who is aware of your actions. You deprive me when you stop being negative; it's your negativity that gives me my energy. And I have to tell you—your selfishness, anger, and jealousy always hit my sweet spot. Take those away from me and malnourishment is guaranteed to follow.

This notion of your feeding me all my power is not a new one. There have been clues throughout history as to how to beat me, but no one has paid much mind to them. The ancient language of Aramaic offered up one of the first clues. In Aramaic, the word for *transgression* actually means "transferring." What do you think is being transferred? The answer: The ultimate food, the ultimate life-sustainer—the Light of the Creator.

And to where is it being transferred? To the dimension where I live.

Yes, I live off Light, just like you.

When the Creator allowed me to roam your dimension, he gave me a limited amount of Light so that I would have just enough power to do my job. The system he put in place feeds me just enough to sustain me—no more, no less. It's not enough to empower me to do major damage.

So where do world wars, global famine, acts of murder, tsunamis, and child abuse come from? From the power you give me! You feed me every time you transgress; you send Light right to where I live. And it gets to me a hell of a lot faster than UPS could send it!

As you will see in the upcoming chapter, the world is created with Ten Dimensions. The nine Upper Dimensions are where God lives and the Tenth Dimension is where you live. But there is a secret Dimension that very few know about. This special place is reserved just for me and it's known as the Eleventh Dimension.

Every time you act selfishly, every time you withhold your love, every time you fail to see God, you send Light to me in the Eleventh Dimension.

DEVIL'S FOOD CAKE

So, let me make this absolutely clear. Each time you protect me, every time you listen to me, each time you deny that I exist, I seize more power from you. Gratification is my appetizer. Indulgence is my entree. Vanity is my dessert. Denial is my life-force. I coerce you into feeding me all the time. You allow me pleasure every day of the week. You gratify me on the hour. You indulge me every minute. And your cynicism is largely to blame.

All the while, you grow weaker. You darken your life a little more with every egocentric reaction. Then you wonder why chaos and darkness suddenly strike you down.

CRUMBS ON THE FLOOR

You do a good deed. The praise arrives on your doorstep, and you soak it up. Bad move on your part, allowing your ego to be stroked. That's another happy meal for me.

You create something. Maybe you write a book, build a business, invent something, develop a piece of technology, bake a batch of award-winning cookies—I don't care what it is—but let's just say you did a swell job. Congratulations come your way. You're showered with praise. Accolades abound. You make a lot of money—whatever!

My point is this: If you use the money, praise, and accolades to feed your ego, I hijack all the power. You get temporary pleasure, while I get a meal for a lifetime.

Even if you give to a good cause, I get a full course meal if you are giving out of guilt or obligation. Because then you are just reacting again. Get it?

A WORTHWHILE TRANSACTION

There was once a man who was asked—let me rephrase—he was *pressured* to give a lot of money to two orphans. After he gave the money, he felt uncomfortable with his decision (of course, I played a hand in that!). He started to calculate how much was left for him during these difficult times. I got him thinking to himself, "You know what? Maybe someone else should have been asked. Why does it have to be me all the time? Maybe I can go and ask for the money back—if not the whole thing, then at least maybe some of it."

In this case, I was really prospering. Why? Because this man had done his act of sharing half-heartedly, which meant that all of the Light that should have gone to him was coming to me! And since we are talking about helping orphans, we're talking about big, big Light coming my way!

But God could not let this go on, so God intervened by sending in one of his special emissaries. The angel showed up dressed like a wealthy merchant. He said, "I hear that you want your money back. That's not a problem. I will give it to you. Just let me have the Light that you were set to receive from this transaction and I will give you the money."

This unusual request slapped this guy out of the coma I had put him in, and he realized that his true desire was for the Light. The emissary offered even more money, but I had lost my hold on the donor. With a clear mind, he was able to affirm that what he wanted was the Light. The money no longer held value for him. And with that, the emissary left.

THE DEVIL INSIDE

Throughout the ages you were given clues. Moses, Jesus, Muhammad, Buddha, and others—they all gave you tools to eradicate me. But naturally, I stepped in. I distorted their teachings. I took their tools and created one of my masterpieces—religion. Unquestionably my greatest invention. Religion protects me. Hides my true identity. Propagates self-righteousness. It keeps you on the straight and narrow—as in *narrow-mindedness*!

Let me tell you a funny story about the nature of religion.

Two monks were walking in the wilderness when all at once they spotted a beautiful woman stranded on the other side of a stream. The young monk was taken aback by her beauty, but didn't skip a beat. Without hesitation, he waded through the stream to assist her. This didn't go over well with his fellow monk. In fact, this is where I step into the story. I planted feelings of disgust in his mind, and the next thing you know he was shouting, "What do you think you are doing?" He watched as the helpful monk lifted the young lady into his arms, carried her safely to the other side, and continued on his way.

The distraught monk crossed the stream, caught up to his helpful colleague, and the two walked side by side without speaking. Some two hours later, the distraught monk said to his friend, "I don't understand how you could have touched that woman, let alone held her in your arms as you carried her across the stream."

The young monk answered, "It's funny that you should say that. I left that woman behind hours ago. It appears that you are still carrying her."

He was right, and it couldn't have happened without me. I linger in the minds of the righteous, encouraging them to blindly adhere to dogma and doctrine while forgetting their real purpose. Like the distraught monk, you blame an external devil for all the problems of the world. But, as you are learning, the true Adversary has taken up residence inside you.

The truth of the matter is that all of you (even the worst of you) are decent, loving people. Deep inside, that is. Your only mistake is you confuse me with you. Want to remove the evil from the world? Want to live forever? Come clean. Right now. End my reign. But know that I'm working hard to make that thought too frightening to even consider.

And to all you folks who flock to houses of worship all over the globe, I have a news flash:

God does not need your worship.

Going to church, synagogue, or the mosque has never been God's goal for you. These are merely places where you can begin the work. Don't get me wrong. Doing your due diligence on Sunday morning isn't a bad thing; just don't think that walking through that door will get me off your back. In fact, I suggest you lose the term altogether: House of Worship. What kind of God would demand that?

It's a trick. A fraudulent understanding (thanks to me) of what is required of you. You are here to wage war, not to worship. The war is against me, the *Satan*. Walk into your place of connection—your mosque, your church, your synagogue—with your ugliest traits fully exposed. Make yourself vulnerable. And use the tools you've been given to wipe me out. The more negativity you admit to and identify as having adopted as your own, the weaker I become.

Life is not about your redeeming qualities. And it's certainly not about your kind personality. Far from it, people.

Life is about your wickedness. Your so-called sins. It's about uncovering all your egocentric traits. In other words, the key to life is finding me inside you. How ironic. The world constantly searches for God in an attempt to find happiness. Big mistake! The search for happiness begins with the search for me! Ferreting out Satan is the path to the Light. Who would've believed it, right?

Did you know that the Latin word *Lucifer*, another name for me, means "Light-bringer" (from *lux/lucis*, meaning "Light," and *ferre*, meaning "to bear/bring")? It doesn't mean "Dark-bringer." Surprised? I've been telling you since the first page of this autobiography that the ultimate truth of my existence is not what you think it is. Not at all.

Think of it this way: A lamp illuminates a room. But then someone lays several blankets over the lampshade, turning the room pitch-black. You walk in and the door slams shut behind you. You can't see a thing, but there's no sense looking for the light switch. The light is already on! Instead, you need to find the blankets that are blocking it.

I cannot make it any simpler than this. The more quickly you remove the blankets, the more quickly the room goes from dark to light. God works the same way. God's Light is always turned on, God's Energy is always present. But there are blankets concealing the Light and I add one every time you serve me. So, find me and you find the Light. Find me, and you find God. Find me, and you find happiness.

Wipe out all the traits I encourage you to take on. Admit your faults, expose your dirty laundry, and reveal your darkest secrets. If you can do that, you leave no place for me to hide.

Know that I will fight you every step of the way. I am supposed to, remember? I will use promotions, and honors, and prizes to celebrate all your wonderful attributes. To celebrate your genius. Your goodness. Your incredible talents. The result? Your self-importance grows and my power over you grows along with it.

So, please continue to sweep the corruption of religion and the ills of society under the carpet. Ignore the abuses of power and the persecution. Instead, walk around telling everyone how good you are. How kind you are. How right you are. How perfect you are. Keep denying that I exist. Wallow in your sense of helplessness. Bask in your depression. Enjoy!

Or get real.

What'll it be?

CHAPTER SIX:

A GARDEN PARTY ATOM & EVE

A HOAX IN EDEN

We touched on Creation in Chapter Two, but let's take a closer look at our humble beginnings. There are some things you need to know regarding the whole Garden of Eden debacle. I think there's a sub-plot in that story that usually gets overlooked.

The Creator conceived you in a supremely luminous and perfect reality. But you were practically unconscious. Why? Utter perfection was all you knew. You had no frame of reference by which to appreciate the life that was handed to you on a silver platter. So, you packed your bags and went on a road trip. You wanted to experience lack so that you could appreciate what you were given.

You wanted to earn the Light that was being handed to you.

And God understood this perfectly. After all, God is the king of unconditional love, right? God respected your desire to leave home; God knew you needed to spend time living bare-bones, roughing it, living hand to mouth. God knew that your separating was an inevitable and necessary step in the process. How else could you learn to cease taking all that you had for granted?

And so, like any good parent, God gave you some advice. Not only should you take an extra pair of clean socks, but God said it was absolutely imperative that you stay away from all selfish indulgences. They would just undermine the whole purpose of your journey, resulting in an even longer and far more painful expedition. Not to mention they would delay your return home. God cautioned you one last time against accepting any kind of short-term pleasure in place of the real thing. He reiterated emphatically:

Don't touch the stuff,
no matter what!

Three very important words.

You understood. And you left.

ROAD TRIP

Your first stop on the trip was to another reality, deep in the subatomic realm. Of course there's no physicality at this level of existence (scientists and I concur on this one), so you didn't bother bringing along your favorite jeans. In this immaterial dimension of existence, you were only a rarified state of consciousness. Here only the *idea* of jeans exists.

This pure force of consciousness consisted not only of you, but of all consciousness. This single super-consciousness gave rise to Adam and Eve. And the dimension in which this unified force of consciousness resided is known as the Garden of Eden.

While you were out enjoying the scenery, God was missing you terribly. And He wanted to give you the chance to come home ASAP. So, God came up with an idea. Instead of your having to go through a long painful journey, God created me to test you without you even knowing it. God's ingenious plan would allow you to resist pleasure and get you back home in time for the holidays. From this good-willed action on the part of God, I, *Satan*, was born. Feel free to join in:

Happy birthday to you, happy birthday to you, happy birthday dear Satan, happy birthday to you!

I was created to challenge your consciousness. The test? You either overcome my temptation for immediate gratification and pleasure, as God asked you to do before you left the house, or you succumb to my powers of persuasion and thus prolong your wandering.

Here's how it all played out.

I pointed out to you an indescribably pleasurable fruit hanging from a tree (I don't have to tell you that it was not a physical fruit, like an apple; we're talking about a reality made of consciousness, pure energy).

You refused. You remembered that God told you not to indulge in any pleasure until you returned home—no matter what.

I then told you that the fruit on the tree was not just some ordinary, run-of-the-mill fruit. It was sure to be a real treat. Why? It tasted just like the fruit waiting for you at home.

But you realized that the whole purpose of your journey was to avoid pleasure in order to appreciate it. And then I explained the following to you: I told you that God sent this fruit as a test to help you. This was true. I told you that all you had to do was resist all selfish desire before tasting it. If you ate it for the sake of making God happy, you would pass the test and your road trip would be over.

I then told you to take a bite. You pushed back. You told me that God said not to taste any pleasure until you returned home—no matter what! I responded by telling you that you had misunderstood the message. God wanted you to come home provided there was a way to achieve it. Removing all selfish desire—before you tasted that fruit—would be a painful enough action to make you worthy of returning home. Now I had your full attention.

I told you that if you ate unselfishly you would pass the test. And you would not be transported to some far-off, God-forsaken region of reality to continue your wandering. The truth of my words rose up inside of you.

You focused. Like a laser. You concentrated all your effort to remove every ounce of self-centered desire from your being. Then, you took a bite. And it worked. Nothing bad happened. On the contrary, you were engulfed with indescribable pleasure.

And that, boys and girls, is the precise moment that I, *Satan*, was placed inside you.

Before you had taken a bite from the fruit, I was a force that existed outside of you. But once you ate from the proverbial apple, I was injected, like a virus, into you. And you didn't know what hit you. In fact, when I first started whispering to you, you panicked; you thought you were schizophrenic, hearing voices. I calmed you down and convinced you I was just the voice of reason inside of you. But I was really mixing truth with lies to deceive you, and to steer you away from the original plan.

Once I was inside of you, you began to feel sick over what you had done. The shame was overpowering. And once you experienced that shame, I owned you. You were mine. At that moment, you disconnected from the Light that was once all you knew. You left the Garden of Eden. You were not kicked out, as you have been led to believe; the shame was so intense, you chose to leave.

As you can imagine, from that point, my influence grew like an unchecked tumor. And just like that, I became the dominant consciousness occupying your brain, the real you concealed behind the curtains and the disgrace I put in your head. This, my friends, was the birth of low self-esteem, my tried-and-true weapon against you.

And this is why you have no idea that I exist, and why you believe you and I are one and the same. You think your selfish thoughts are you, and that's why you give up. Once you truly know it's me, and not you, you will be able to fight me; you will be secure enough to share. You will know that you are like God.

BIRTH OF HUMANITY

The task of overcoming me was almost too great to achieve once I had become so entrenched within you. God saw this and, although he promised not to interfere, he decided to split up the workload. The one super-consciousness of Adam and Eve was disassembled into countless smaller particles of consciousness. These became the building blocks of the entire cosmos. They created everything, from the human body to the selfish survival instinct that governs the entire human race.

Once you triumph over this preprogrammed consciousness, you will conquer death and return home—which simply means that happiness will be yours forever. Home is not in some far-away dimension. Home is a state of unending happiness. And that is what God is. Nothing more. Nothing less.

SECOND CHANCES

God created a way for you to make up for what you did, to grow from your mistake—to feel worthy when you feel like nothing.

God wanted to show you how strong you are and how much you are really capable of.

God wanted you to increase the size of your Vessel, to grow your potential so you could have so much more.

God wanted you to cleanse and remove the blocks I created when I entered your psyche.

How did God set out to accomplish this feat?

By testing you. And by enlisting me to be the Teacher's Aide.

CHAPTER SEVEN:

YOU ARE BEING TESTED

I can feel your anxiety building now, like that nightmare where you walk into a classroom completely unprepared for the exam. Relax. Remember, I am divulging all my secrets here so you can better prepare this time around. Test preparation is the name of the Game.

I'd like to take a minute to familiarize you with the classroom and the rules that govern this space. First off, know that you'll never get a test that you can't handle. The universe has equipped you with all of the tools you'll need to ace every exam that comes your way.

There are two important things to keep in mind:

1. Within every test, always be on the lookout for me. Think of each test as a page from *Where's Waldo*? I'll always be there somewhere. Need a clue? Where selfishness is rearing its pretty head, you are sure to find me.

2. Think of the other person.

With any test you encounter, let me tell you that the odds are in your favor. But just because God is on your side doesn't mean you should ever ask to be tested. Ask for a test and the odds change big-time. Talk about *Ask and You Shall Receive!* I'll enter your consciousness with a force you are not prepared to handle. Only God knows when you are ready, so let God decide when to send me in to do my job.

And God will. Because God knows that you cannot increase the size of your Vessel without tests. You can't go back to Kansas without confronting the wicked witch that is your selfish nature.

TWO TYPES

I will tell you this much: There are two types of tests I might throw your way. There's the One Shot Deal: Blow it and you're done. And the other is my personal favorite: The Slow Burn.

Just the mere sound of these brings me great excitement. With the One Shot Deal, my goal is to hit you with one singular life experience that packs such a powerful punch it leaves you shattered under the sheer "unfairness" of it all.

The Slow Burn speaks for itself. With this test, I wear you down slowly. Over time, I corrupt your consciousness. You don't even know that it's happening! It's like the frog in the boiling water experiment. Drop a frog into a pot of nice, cool water and then gradually bring that water to a boil. Then, sit back as the frog cooks up nice and hearty. But if you drop that same frog into a pot of boiling water, he'll jump ship in a heartbeat. In that same way, I prefer the oh-so-slow-and-steady line of attack. It takes a great deal of patience on my part, but the payoff is that you never see it coming.

By the way, I will never let you know the weight of the test in the big picture. You will never know if you are taking a final exam or a mere quiz. So, beware. Sometimes, a small test is really a big test in disguise. I freely admit it—I'm a sucker for disguises.

POP QUIZZES VERSUS TESTS

On the flip side, sometimes you think you're being given the ultimate test, but the truth is that it's hardly a test at all—call it a pop quiz, at best. Say you're out of town on a business trip and an attractive business associate asks you to join him in his room later. You decline and walk away, proud of yourself for resisting such a tempting offer. But how great was the temptation really? You have a wonderful spouse at home, great kids, and a comfortable life. You might have been flattered by the offer, but turning it down didn't cost you much. That doesn't mean that you passed the test; it just means that it wasn't much of a test in the first place. Or maybe it was another kind of test. Where am I hiding? In the pride? In the righteousness?

On the other hand, if in that same scenario, it takes every ounce of willpower to force the word *no* from your lips as you fantasize about what you'll be missing, then congratulations—now, you are starting to play every bit as hard as I do. See, it's not about the sex that you are choosing to have or not have; it's about the degree to which you recognize and overcome me, your selfish nature.

Performing well on one of my many tests is rarely as simple as choosing one action over another, and it's never about right and wrong. It's about what your choice means to you. If I could give you a foolproof rule to go by, that would be too easy, wouldn't it? That's not how I play the Game.

The key to giving me a real challenge is to be aware that every moment offers an opportunity. Everything starts with awareness. Sure, it sounds simple. But becoming aware is never easy with the likes of me around, and that's the way it's meant to be. I hide inside every minute of your life. So, look out and wake up. Or pay the piper.

YOU WILL FAIL

No one is ever going to pass every test all the time. It's the practice that makes for perfection, remember? To win, you have to fail a few times. It's like the major league batter who makes it into the Hall of Fame for hitting 700 home runs in his career. Imagine how many times the guy swung and missed, fouled out, or was thrown out? Yet, he's one of the best in the history of the game!

Sure, it's easy for baseball players because they know what they need to do. Hit it out of the park, right? But I make it much harder for you to keep your eyes on the prize and your head in the Game. But if you can overcome *me* located inside of you and learn to appreciate that paradise and the Garden are your destiny, you're home free.

You will suffer mistakes and misfires. Your job is to refuse to get bogged down by them. That is to say, failure is part of the journey. Failure is part of the grand design; it's an integrated component on the motherboard of life. You can't simply remove it or the function it serves.

In fact, the only real failure comes when you fail to grow from the challenges you come up against. Real success, on the other hand, is falling down, dusting yourself off, and getting right back into the fray. If you buy into my lie that you have failed, you have committed the ultimate sin.

And what's the consequence of committing the ultimate sin? Immediate death by lightning bolt? An eternity in Dante's Inferno? I admit that drama and theatrics are normally my style, so it might surprise you that the price for buying into this myth comes without much theatrical fanfare. It's pretty simple, really.

When you believe you are a failure, you sacrifice joy. You forfeit fulfillment. And you say good-bye to any chance at peace of mind. That is the consequence of the ultimate sin. It doesn't look so bad on paper, but, in reality, it's hell.

But there is some good news here. There is an alternative. And it's called letting go.

Let go of the ego, and I'll let go of you.

I'll let you keep the happiness and fulfillment that is your birthright if you will let go of the notion that you are not worthy of having this joy. When you let go of me, I let go of you. It's a powerful Game we are playing. And you are playing against the master. Are you having fun yet?

CHAPTER EIGHT:
MEASURE FOR MEASURE

Pay close attention because the more quickly you catch on to this next idea, the less explaining I'll have to do. There is a process—a system—for everything in the universe. One of the most important principles in this system is something I call *Measure for Measure*, and it goes something like this:

- To the extent that you judge others, you will be judged.
- To the extent that you love others, you will be loved.
- To the extent that you care, you will be cared for.
- To the extent that you hate, you will be hated.
- To the extent that you envy, you will be envied.

Catching on? There's a one-to-one ratio—a direct correlation—between the thoughts and actions that you direct toward others and the thoughts and actions that are directed at you. You don't have to be a mathematician to understand this Universal Law. But you do need to pay attention.

The way this principle works is not personal in any way. It is simply a spiritual law of our universe that is every bit as straightforward as the physical laws which govern space. Just as the law of gravity doesn't take into account the personality of the individual who gets hit in the head by a coin dropped from the top of a skyscraper, neither does the principle of Measure for Measure vary by individual. It's not about feelings or personalities; it's about spiritual energy.

For every action, there is a directly proportional reaction. When you hurl a ball against a wall, it comes back to you with the exact same force. In the same way, the universe throws back to you, pound for pound, exactly that which you throw at it.

The system is perfect and impersonal, and it's not limited to you and your actions. The balance of humankind is also determined by the Measure for Measure principle. Just like you, the world is always being tested. Just like you, it evolves and grows from its experiences and then is challenged again by something new. Just like you, humankind as a whole has selfish attributes it has come here to correct, attributes which must be turned into Light before the world's consciousness can advance to the next level.

You don't have to look hard to find examples of the world being pushed to its limits by the likes of me. The shattered state of the environment, the depressed global economy, unpredictable foreign relations, war-ravaged nations, widespread famine, and the AIDS crisis—I've been hard at work lately. Such large-scale negativity helps you completely forget about sharing and removing selfishness. Heck, it leaves you totally dumbstruck.

But it gets even better. Everything you allow me to do to you personally is magnified on a global scale. Every negative thought adds to the suffering of the world. My insidious nature can prove devastating if you let it.

But only if you let it: Underneath my dazzling shows of death and destruction lies the possibility for immeasurable Light to be revealed by the human spirit. Without my little tests, you would never discover your greatness. Coming face-to-face with a gut-wrenching challenge reveals a degree of strength inside of you that you didn't even know you had. These tests, whether they are individual or global, help build you into the person you were meant to be. The tests you come up against help to expand your

Vessel, thereby creating an opening for Light. In fact, every ounce of God-inspired potential you were granted upon your soul's creation becomes activated when you pass one of my endless stream of tests.

If you were never tested, not only would you be stuck with a constant feeling of being unfulfilled, but there would be no mechanism for removing blockages from your past—for clearing away the garbage that you carry with you from one lifetime to the next. By passing tests, you change the course of your destiny.

That's what happened to Rav Akiva's daughter. Rav Akiva lived a long time ago and, being a kabbalist, was a real thorn in my side. He certainly was someone who understood the significance of my grueling tests.

RAV AKIVA'S DAUGHTER

On the day his daughter was born, astrologers informed Rav Akiva that his daughter would die on her wedding day. Knowing this, he prepared his daughter well. He taught her much of the same wisdom I am sharing with you in this book: The dangers of selfishness, the necessity of sharing, and the secret ways I operate. Needless to say, with an upbringing like that, this was a woman who was prepared to be tested.

On the evening of her wedding, she decided to take off the brooch which adorned her dress and stick it to the wall so she wouldn't lose it. But unbeknownst to her, the pin of her brooch went through the thin wall and lodged in the eye of the serpent I had sent to kill her. It wasn't until the next morning when she pulled the pin out of the wall that she found the dead snake. Despite the predictions to the contrary, Rav Akiva's daughter had survived her wedding day—untouched by me or my agents.

As you can imagine, Rav Akiva was both elated and curious to know how his daughter had averted death. He asked his daughter if anything out of the ordinary had happened to her before her nuptials. His daughter explained that a poor man had come into the banquet hall in need of a meal, and she had given him food. What seemed like a simple gesture of sharing was in reality one of my most demanding tests. Why? Because, according to custom, the bride had fasted on the day leading up to her wedding night. So, choosing to share her first meal in 24 hours was no small thing! As it turned out, her decision to share changed the poor man's destiny and her own. Had it not been for her father's coaching, and the consciousness that inspired her to share, she would not have passed my test. She would have died, and the man would have gone hungry.

Absolutely everyone gets tested, and absolutely everyone is subject to the Measure for Measure principle. Rich or poor. Educated or unschooled. Good or evil. These qualifiers mean nothing in the realm of spiritual law. A smart man's business crashes and he loses everything, while an illiterate man wins the lottery. Even the most righteous will get tested. In the eyes of the Creator, it all makes perfect sense.

HE WHO JUDGES

As much as I hate to admit it, there are people throughout history who had my number. The Creator sent them as a way to level the playing field. Rav Isaac Luria was one of my greatest adversaries. Why? Because Rav Isaac Luria understood the big picture, which means he understood me. Let me tell you a true story.

THE BAKER AND THE BEGGAR

There once was a baker who lived in a small town. One Friday afternoon, he decided that he wanted to do something special for the Creator to show his appreciation for the many blessings in his life. Obviously, this was not a thought inspired by me. In fact, this baker was a man of so much Light that it was next to impossible for me to influence him in any way.

The baker baked some of his best bread and took it with him to the temple. As he stood before the Ark, I heard him say, "God, please accept this sacrifice. I want to be closer to you." Was this guy pure Light or what? He placed the bread inside the Ark and left.

Five minutes later, a beggar walked into the temple. He was so hungry that he went to the Ark and began to cry like a baby. I heard him pleading, "Please, God, help me."

I had to stick around for this.

When he opened the Ark, he discovered the two loaves of bread left behind by the baker. Believing that they had been delivered straight from the Creator himself, the beggar was elated, to say the least. Not only did he have food to eat, but the Creator obviously deemed him worthy enough to receive the bread—or so he believed.

The next morning, I watched as the baker returned to the temple to see if God had accepted his gift. Indeed, the bread was gone, and the baker was beside himself with joy at having been of service to the Creator. What could I do? Absolutely nothing. I was powerless.

A week later, the baker brought more bread to the Ark, and the same thing happened. The beggar took the loaves without hesitation. This went on, week after week, year after year, until 14 years had passed.

For 14 years, I was unable to penetrate this Light. Then, one Friday afternoon, I encouraged the clergyman of the temple to fall into a deep sleep. He was awoken by the sound of someone opening a door. When he looked into the sanctuary, he saw the baker put the bread into the Ark and leave. A few minutes later, the beggar entered, took the loaves out of the Ark, and ran away.

After watching this scene, I saw my "in"—the clergyman! Talk about a man full of self-righteousness. So, I put thoughts of disgust into his head. Easy as pie. "I will fix this," I encouraged him to think to himself.

The following day, the clergyman called the baker and the beggar into his office. Again, I took charge:

> *What do the two of you think you're doing here? One of you puts the bread in, and the other one takes it out. The one fantasizes that he's working with God, and the other is just a common thief. God is not involved in this transaction at all! You have no business coming to this sanctuary. Stay out!*

At that very second, the great sage, Rav Isaac Luria, came in and saw me there. Talk about being caught red-handed! He saw my selfishness and ego with absolute clarity. This wise man turned to the clergyman and said, "Prepare yourself to die. The Angel of Death has you, and you are going to leave this world before the end of the day."

Sure enough, I took that poor clergyman's mortal life by sunset.

True story.

Here's what the clergyman refused to see, and why he failed this important test: God *was* involved—intimately involved. It was no coincidence that for 14 years, the baker always arrived just before the beggar. Never once did they come in the wrong order, or at the wrong time.

How did this happen? The Creator was so happy with what he saw in this simple unconditional exchange between baker and beggar that the temple was filled with incredible Light—Light that I could not corrupt or compromise. For 14 years, this Light had kept the beggar alive, for that first day he came weeping to the Ark was the very day I had been planning to take him.

You see, the clergyman had to learn the lesson the hard way. Judgment only manifests when someone activates it by placing judgment on someone else. Had it not been for me and my influence, the clergyman would have seen the larger picture and chosen to share tolerance instead of judgment. But he didn't pass the test.

The ways in which I will test you will push you far beyond your comfort zone. But you can handle it, especially if you're paying close enough attention to what I'm telling you. And you can start preparing right now by imagining how my tests might appear in your life. If you tend to be envious, for example, your test will involve overcoming envy. If you have been judgmental, it's a guarantee that someday you will be asked to forgo your judgment. And that quick wit that you pride yourself on? Know that at some point in the not-so-distant future, your test will be to hold your sharp tongue and offer unconditional acceptance instead.

Every test I send your way is perfectly designed for you. So, as much as you might prefer to dodge the consequences of your thoughtless actions, it's impossible, spiritually speaking. You can't wave a magic wand in the hope that your poor choices or their results will magically disappear. You get precisely what you give, for better and for worse.

One final note on this topic: The tests you take are constantly evolving along with you. A test that you took yesterday will not look like one you take today. Each test is in perfect alignment with the person you are today. Call it a spiritual curriculum that is custom-made for you. And it's all free of charge.

CHAPTER NINE:

THE REVELATION REVISITED

MOUNT SINAI

Let's revisit the site of the most famous event in the history of the Judeo-Christian world—the Revelation on Mount Sinai. Since I am trying to reach the widest possible audience with this, my first public communication with humanity, I will summarize the traditional Sunday-school version of the story of Moses and the Ten Commandments for those not familiar with it. Academics, scholars, and religious fanatics, bear with me.

Here's how the story goes: 3400 years ago, 600,000 Israelites were slaves in the land of Egypt. God sent a man by the name of Moses to free the Israelites. Moses led them on a journey out of Egypt through the desert all the way to Mount Sinai. Moses climbed the mountain while the Israelites set up camp. God gave Moses two stone tablets inscribed with the Ten Commandments. While Moses was away, the Israelites began to party. Their clubbing made the wildest raves of the eighties and nineties look like a Victorian tea party by comparison.

But after a while, the Israelites began to panic. They worried that Moses might not come back. So they swiped some gold jewelry from the other clubbers, melted it down, and fashioned it into a statue of a golden calf, a molten god to replace Moses as the intermediary to the Divine Force. To their surprise, Moses returned with the Tablets. When he saw the golden calf, along with all the hung-over Israelites, he was a little peeved, to say the least. So, he smashed the Tablets. With that, what's known as the Revelation Event came to an end.

Moses went back up the mountain to retrieve a second set of Tablets, which were then placed in what is known as the Ark of the Covenant. The whole story of Moses was then inscribed into what you now call The Old Testament, or Bible. Included in the Bible are the Ten Commandments—a supposed ethical, moralistic code for living—which comprise "Thou Shalt Not Kill," "Thou Shalt Not Steal," and the like.

That's generally how the story goes, right?

What's missing is the story *behind* the story.

THE REAL STORY AND THE HIDDEN TEST

First off, the event on Mount Sinai was really a test to give you a chance to make up for what took place in the Garden of Eden, to give you an opportunity to earn your way back to paradise. By the way, if you haven't figured it out by now, the people of Mount Sinai share the same souls as Adam and Eve, just as you do. And you are all trying to find your way back home.

Here's what really happened: Moses told you to wait here while he went back up the mountain to seal the deal with God. That's all you had to do. He told you to demonstrate a little bit of patience. Wait. No matter what! Just wait. But, no. You didn't listen to Moses. You listened to me instead. I showed up as every negative emotion that welled up inside of you. This time, I stepped in as impatience, fear, and anxiety.

You were duped by me again, and the golden calf was built.

Now, if you read the story as code for the story within, you can see that God was setting you up for victory. The potent combination of Moses eradicating his ego and you battling me down at the bottom of the mountain by resisting impatience and selfish partying would have been enough to bring an end to my reign over humanity. Moses did his part, but you didn't do yours. You only had to experience the brief pain of resisting your impatience until Moses came back.

That was all you had to do.

But you refused to accept that pain. You chose pleasure instead. Sex. Drugs. Rock 'n' roll. You turned it into a real orgy. Moses got to the Light by considering the needs of others. You rejected the Light of Mount Sinai by considering your own needs above those of others.

The truth is that I tricked you into believing Moses might not be coming back. I made you anxious and impatient. I encouraged you to act prematurely. I got you worried about losing that high, that connection to the Light. The golden calf was your shortcut to feeling good.

And you're still doing the same thing today, only today's golden calves are not statues. They are the drugs that make you feel good, the celebrities you place on pedestals, the marketing that you buy into, the plastic surgery you just can't live without, the diets, the empty glitter.... Do I need to go on? The golden calf of today is anything that makes you feel good for the moment, anything that you don't have to work for, anything that, at the end of the day, makes you feel less worthy and more disconnected from God—more like the slave you have become.

Face it, every day you give your power to the golden calf. Every day, you bank on the fact that something other than God will bring you joy. You believe that happiness comes from this money or that thing or this person instead of knowing with certainty that it can only come from the Light.

When you choose the golden calf, you forgo immortality. You take an apple from the Tree of Knowledge, instead of from the Tree of Eternal Life. And that's what you did on Mount Sinai. You took the easy way out. You chose the quick path to the Light, instead of waiting for the real deal. You chose an external high over eternal bliss. Granted, it was I who offered you that option. And that was the test. The test you failed. You weren't prepared, just as you weren't prepared in the Garden of Eden; you weren't ready.

More specifically, you weren't prepared to battle me and the powerful force of impatience I employed. But had you been able to resist the urge to react, you would have earned all the Light and energy that Moses was bringing down from the Mountain. I would have been banished forever from the landscape of human civilization! Instead, you tried to connect to all Ten Dimensions before you eradicated me from your nature. That was your downfall.

When Moses broke the Tablets, it was a symbol. It meant your connection to the Hidden Dimensions was broken. Severed and shattered. And you know what happened next? Death was reborn.

And something else was born on that day.

Any guesses?

Religion.

THE CHARADE

I'll come totally clean. There were no Commandments on Mount Sinai. I'm serious. The whole notion of a Commandment? My idea. Honest. If you check the Old Testament in its original Hebrew, you will see it says God spoke Ten Utterances on Mount Sinai; God never gave Ten Commandments.

Here's one of my best-kept secrets: God does not command, nor does God punish. And the Lord of all Creation most definitely does not reward. Those are my creations as well. I invented those concepts and slipped them into your religious belief systems.

Do you really believe that an all-loving God would punish you for making an honest mistake? Or that God would dump you into a world where you're punished for yielding to temptation? Especially when the deck has been stacked against you from the moment you were born?

Is that your God? No. It's me disguised as God. It's the God I invented to prevent you from knowing the real God. The real God doesn't punish. He doesn't reward. God only shares. Period.

And what he shares is never-ending goodness.

Nothing bad can emerge from a Force of such Light. Nothing. Nor does God pay off for good behavior. God is not a slot machine. And God doesn't penalize you for sin. The universe isn't the People's Court, and God is not Judge Judy.

God simply is!

And the "is" is only good. Kind. Loving. Pleasurable. Idyllic. Overwhelmingly delightful.

THE INVISIBLE MAN

A wise old invisible man? With a long, flowing beard? And a shining robe? Sitting on a heavenly throne? It's an absurdity. I'm sorry to burst your bubble, but how can an infinite Divine Force possibly fit inside a finite physical body? I fed you those harebrained anthropomorphic images to prevent you from finding out the truth. And what's the truth?

God is a brilliant all-pervading Force of limitless energy. Period. And this Force consists of infinite, endless happiness, wisdom, and goodness—beyond human comprehension. There is nothing negative or evil or judgmental within this Force. Nothing.

Too abstract? Can't wrap your head around it? Look at the force of electricity. It's everywhere. In the walls. The air. Running through your body. Electricity doesn't punish, penalize, or reward. If you plug a computer into an outlet and pocket a few thousand dollars selling goods on eBay, you feel pretty good. But stick your finger into the same socket and you're toast. But who in their right mind would say the electrical current deliberately rewarded or punished you? The electricity never changed. Electricity just is!

The way you connect to this powerful unseen, odorless, invisible force determines whether the result is positive some money in the bank—or negative—Kentucky Fried Finger.

THE GOD CURRENT

The infinite Force that you call God operates the very same way. God is not an invisible man in Heaven. The word *God* refers to an infinite pure Force of Sharing Consciousness. This Force maintains the entire universe. Every molecule, every atom, every subatomic particle is sustained by this unseen Force. This Energy is also the absolute, ultimate source of all wisdom. Happiness. Knowledge. Joy. Healing. Prosperity. And life.

IT'S ONLY YOU

Listen up: God didn't cause your chaos. You did. Your behavior is the Cause. But you don't often see the connection between Cause and Effect because I blind you with the illusion of randomness. Chance. Luck.

But I have some news: Luck is a lie. Within the chaos of life lies impeccable order. But you cannot even fathom, for one moment, that your behavior toward your fellow man is the sole Cause of both the blessings and the mayhem that you attract in life. Human behavior is the Cause of all ills. Global and personal. Even when nature strikes back with an earthquake, or a tsunami, the Cause is human behavior.

You don't see it. You can't accept it. It sounds too simple. But the truth is that "Love Thy Neighbor" is a magnificent piece of technology. It's all you need for creating a world of perfect order. Trust me.

Now that you understand the true lesson of punishment and reward, let me reveal the even deeper story behind Moses and the Ten Utterances. I've hoodwinked you for 34 centuries, so it's about time I let you in on the secret.

THE PRISCA THEOLOGIA: THE SECRET WISDOM

A very long time ago, roughly 3400 years, the collective souls of humanity dug themselves into a deep hole. Very deep. For centuries, they lived only to gratify their primal selfish desires. I owned them. This is the slavery that was taking place in the Bible story of the Israelites in Egypt. The story of the Israelites enslaved in Egypt really refers to the fact that all humanity was enslaved by me. And this life of slavery was all these souls knew.

Consequently, humankind was on the verge of disconnecting completely from the Source. The planet was facing total destruction. So God stepped in and threw you a lifeline again. He revealed a technology and wisdom (not a religion) that would allow the entire planet to plug back into the electrical current called

God. At the very least, it would put you back on equal footing with me. At best, it would deliver paradise, immortality, and the demise of yours truly.

What is that technology and secret wisdom? Where is it? Only a few great souls in every generation have known about it. Sir Isaac Newton, Plato, and Pythagoras knew. So did Theophilus Gale, the renowned 17th century philosopher. Add Jonathan Edwards, America's most fiery theologian, to the list. And the infamous Count of Mirandola, also known as Giovanni Pico, a great Christian mystic and a man of enormous intellectual power. Gottfried Leibniz, inventor of calculus during the Renaissance, also understood this technology.

These men believed that all the world's wisdom, including religious wisdom, Greek philosophy, and science, had its roots in the secret wisdom given to Moses on Mount Sinai. They called it *Prisca Theologia*, which means "the most ancient theology," or "primordial wisdom." It was a universal knowledge that had the power to transform the world, unite all of humanity, and rid the world of my influence. In Aramaic, it is called the "Wisdom of Truth."

You can imagine that I had to make sure most people never caught on to this idea. So I twisted it, corrupted it, and made sure you called it religion. But Newton and company understood that organized religion was never part of the deal at Mount Sinai. Never.

I am not saying the Bible is false. I am simply saying that the true meaning of the Bible is hidden, by design, underneath the literal text. To find it, you've got to do a little digging, some searching and studying. Throughout history, I convinced you that there was no hidden meaning behind the Bible. I told you to follow it literally. Blindly. And you listened. In fact, many of you right now will have a difficult time believing this. But that's your problem. I am just doing my job.

But many of the most brilliant thinkers in history, from Newton to Plato, knew there was a *Prisca Theologia*, a secret wisdom that unlocks the hidden truths of the Bible.

THE WAY OF SPIRITUAL WISDOM

When you grasp the *Prisca Theologia*, the inner meaning of a biblical text, the Bible does something quite remarkable. It unleashes Divine Forces that can transform your world by transforming you. Specifically, each time you find a secret inside the Bible, that wisdom eradicates a measure of my influence from your life.

That is the only reason to learn the *Prisca Theologia*. It's not to become wiser or intellectually superior. It's about becoming better able to handle the tests, so you can limit my influence on your consciousness. And as I become less powerful, all the peoples of the world will come to recognize their unity; they will come to know that I, alone, was behind all the hatred, conflict, war, and dying that took place across the landscape of human civilization. Through the *Prisca Theologia*—the hidden wisdom—the Bible becomes a path to immortality and eternal happiness.

If, however, you read the Bible literally, it becomes a force for death. Having a hard time believing that? You think it's a coincidence that for 2000 years, more killings have taken place in the name of religion than from any other single cause? The Bible is like electricity. Study it literally, and you've got your finger in the socket. Probe its hidden meaning, and the electricity lights up your life!

This is why the great minds of history searched the world for the secrets locked in the Bible. Newton. The Knights Templar. Pythagoras. Did they find it? I will not tell you. You've got to earn the Light yourself. But I can share a few encoded secrets in the story of Moses and the Ten Commandments. That much I can do for you.

I'll begin with the Ten Utterances.

THE TEN UTTERANCES

This world is where I test you. This world is where you are given the opportunity to turn darkness into Light, self-loathing into acceptance, and shame into love. This world is your chance to go back to the Garden. That's the way it has been set up. But, as I've mentioned, there are nine other Dimensions beyond this physical reality. You can't experience them with your five senses, but they are the source of all goodness. The Light of God fills every corner of these other Dimensions.

Is your Bible still open? If you read *Genesis*, you will see the phrase, "God says," mentioned 10 times. These are the Ten Sayings, or the Ten Utterances. Of course, God does not really say things, at least not in the traditional sense. These Utterances are the code for the Ten Dimensions that I just told you about.

Why do we need all these Dimensions? God needed to cover up his Light in order to create the absence of Light, or darkness. So, God erected ten veils, each one further dimming the Light that radiated from God's being.

Now I am going to do something I never do. I'm going to expose one of my greatest weaknesses. Why now? Because, as I stated earlier, you are at a critical juncture in human history. It's time to level the playing field.

Ready?

Here we go: **I cannot access these Hidden Dimensions**. They're off-limits. I have no power over there. Zero. These Dimensions belong to God, which means that they are precisely where your Source of everything good is hiding.

MY GEOGRAPHICAL BOUNDARIES

I only roam in this world (and in the Eleventh Dimension), where I feed off of your negative energy. Your job is to bypass me and connect to the Hidden Dimensions; that way you'll bring energy into this God-forsaken dark Dimension called Earth. If you can access those Hidden Dimensions, I cannot touch you. I cannot pressure you. I only get one place to play with you: Planet Earth. Yep, this physical reality is it. Hollywood and Vine. 42nd and Broadway. Boulevards Saint-Michel and Saint-Germain. Yonge and

Bloor. Avenidas de Mayo and 9 de Julio, and the Obelisco. The Shibuya Crossing.

My job is to make it difficult for you to enter into the Hidden Dimensions and access the Light. I throw you curveballs, send you on detours, place obstacles before you—all so that you can overcome me and earn your right to reconnect to those Dimensions of Light, the Garden, paradise.

So, we have two realms: A realm of darkness (look around), and a realm of Light composed of Nine Dimensions (look within). Together, they form the Ten. And, this, my friends, is the spiritual system. If you ever intend to beat me, you must know that this system is the key, the gateway, the connection, the way back home to God.

When you know this, it works every time. Not just sometimes. How do you come to know something? Only through personal experience. You can't just take somebody's word for it. You can't just believe in something. You have to *know*. Because knowing something means you're batting 1000. You're 10 for 10. Believing something, on the other hand, means you're batting 200. Two for 10. Who in their right mind wants to choose a life where they are only getting 20 percent of what they want to make them happy?

THE BELIEF GAME

Knowing is at the heart of endless happiness, but you continue to rely on mere belief. Not only that, but you argue over whose belief system is correct.

The Bible, in *Genesis* 4:1, says:

> *"Adam knew Eve and she bore Cain."*

When you read the Bible literally, it sounds like every woman that a man knows will soon be carrying his love child. Ludicrous, I am sure you'll agree.

The *Prisca Theologia* reveals the truth. Adam and Eve are metaphors in this particular passage. Eve is a metaphor for humanity. You! Adam is a metaphor for the Divine Light, the simplest, deepest happiness you could ever imagine. The only way to connect Earth with the Divine, and you with true happiness, is through knowledge. See what's really going on here? When the Bible says, "Adam knew Eve and she bore Cain," the word *knew* is a stand-in for *knowledge*.

KNOWLEDGE IS THE CONNECTION

Knowledge gives you the Universal Rules of the Game of Life. Knowledge allows you to connect yourself to the Divine, to connect yourself to unending contentment. You access the Hidden Dimensions when you pass a test, or grow from a failed test.

Are you starting to get a sense of where this is heading? Darkness and suffering occur when you disconnect yourself from these Hidden Dimensions of Light. It's no different than unplugging a lamp from the wall. Moses made the connection when he overcame me, when he plugged this physical world into the world of Light. That is not to say, he passed all the tests; he didn't, but that is a subject for another book. For the purpose of these pages, let me just say, Moses performed well and he got me good.

All the Dimensions were aligned and connected as one. The Light went back on. Darkness gave way to Light. Death disappeared. The Israelites and all of humanity were free from my clutches. As I revealed earlier, there are no commandments. Moses connected all Ten Dimensions and turned the Light on, and he did so by virtue of his selfless behavior. That was it. No magic. Nothing supernatural. No commandments from God. Moses climbing Mount Sinai is a code for Moses connecting this physical world to the Hidden Source. That's the secret! A secret hidden from the world (by me) for over 34 centuries. Admit it. I did one hell of a job.

THE BLUEPRINT

So, what happened? We know that the story did not end right then and there with paradise becoming the new reality. You saw the Israelites miss their golden opportunity, thanks to my efforts. If they had won, that would have been too easy. The Game was still in its early stages. You need to win this Game for yourself, remember? You have to earn it all on your own. And, trust me, I give you plenty of different ways to make that happen. In fact, in the next part of this book, I'm going to reveal each and every way that I test you, challenge you, and help you to earn your keep in paradise.

So, do me a favor. Don't screw this up, OK? God seems to believe that you can pull it off this time around. Needless to say, I am not so sure! But go ahead and prove me wrong. With the cheat sheet I'm about to give you, you'd have to be an idiot to get it wrong this time.

2

PART II:

THE TESTS

CHAPTER TEN:

TEST NUMBER ONE

CAN YOU TRUST IN YOUR CONNECTION TO GOD (NO MATTER WHAT)?

FALSE IDOLS

Like the Israelites who worshipped the golden calf, you, too, are a slave. Don't even try to deny it. Are you addicted to caffeine, food, sex, or alcohol? Are you at a loss without your internet connection or your TV? If you are, then you are giving your power away. Instead of accessing the Hidden Dimension, which contains every form of fulfillment you can experience, you are looking for the "apple;" you are trusting in fat and sugar, drugs and alcohol, baubles and adrenaline, or any number of other external highs.

You are enslaved because you don't think that God has put a system in place for you to be successful. You don't think God has set you up to win. But God has. And that is your first test: Can you trust in God's system? Can you trust in your connection to God? If you can't, then you're mine. All mine.

THE SYSTEM AT WORK

You'd have to be blind not to see it. Open your eyes! The very planet you live on is part of the most intricate of systems: The Milky Way, the moon, the sun, the relationship of celestial bodies to one another, the rotation of the Earth—it's all perfectly orchestrated. The universe in which you and I operate exists as part of a perfected state, where you live most of your life perfectly unaware. Asleep at the wheel. Sure, over the course of history you've figured out that the Earth isn't flat, and that other galaxies exist beyond this one. Good for you! But you are still oblivious to the larger picture.

As soon as you figure out that there is more to life than what you see, then you're on the path to defeating me. Trust that there is a system in place, even when there is no visible proof. And trust that all of the challenges—all of the tests—that you take on in your life are designed to bring you to your best outcome, even if it doesn't seem that way at the time. Mostly, you lack perspective, because I put blinders on you. But that's what you are here to work on.

All the fears that you experience in life are based on your lack of trust in the bigger picture. Sure, you've got questions. Tons of questions. Sure, you feel alone. And that's all my doing. That's my job. I haven't let you know that you are just one step away from finding the answers, and from feeling completely connected to something wonderfully powerful beyond reason. You're so busy listening to me that you usually give up before you take that last step, before you turn over that last rock.

The truth, if you must know, is that the answer existed before the question. I created the question. The answers were always there, just like God was and is always there. God is the Dimension of answers. Home has all the answers. But you left home to find them for yourself. That's fine and good, but now you aren't even looking for answers. You've settled. You have settled for a life filled with the questions I put in your head. And I'm here to tell you that's a big, big mistake.

Knowing that there is a system allows you to take responsibility for finding the truth. You cease being a victim, a seeker jumping from one cause to the next. I love seekers! But you have to become a finder to beat me.

CHAPTER ELEVEN:
TEST NUMBER TWO
WHO KNOWS BEST? (ANSWER: GOD DOES.)

What would you do if someone in a position of power in your life asked you to walk away from your home, your family, your livelihood, and your community without any guarantee of what would happen next? God sprung this request on Moses, so God might do the same to you. So, what would you do?

I'd bet the farm you'd laugh. I know you would. Why? Because you think you know better. Admit it. I know you do. The very moment you think you need to play know-it-all is precisely the moment you need to just shut up and listen. Do exactly what you are being challenged to do in spite of the fact that you think you know better. Trust me, you don't!

That's because only the Creator has the perspective to know your true purpose and to help you achieve it. You see, you came here to do a specific job, and while my task is to keep you off-track from your true purpose, the Creator is doing everything in the Creator's power to lead you to it. The question is: How long will you let me lead you astray? How long will you deny yourself a life of purpose and fulfillment?

KING DAVID

King David and his best friend Jonathan had it figured out. They didn't give me any way in to ruin their connection with one another, or with the Creator. Maybe you know the story of these two men. If you don't, I'll give you the short version. David was best friends with Jonathan, who was the son of King Saul and the rightful heir to the throne. Both David and Jonathan had such trust of the

Creator, as well as love for each other, that they were both willing to forgo the throne, if necessary, to maintain their friendship.

Can you imagine having that kind of faith in the Creator? That kind of love for another soul? That certainty that the Creator knows best? Can you imagine having the willingness to say, "I am here and I am willing to do what needs to be done?" David was willing to stay or to go. He was willing to leave his best friend and abandon the kingdom based on what God wanted. Just like that. Try that one on for size!

Have you got what it takes?

DO WHAT YOU'RE TOLD

If the universe encourages you to act now, it's in your absolute interest to do so. If the universe makes it clear that you need to stay put, then stay put. For once in your life, don't listen to me.

That means that if you find yourself stuck in Mexico because of a passport issue or some other snafu, know that there is Light to be revealed exactly where you are located—either for you personally or for those around you, or both. Or if you're traveling somewhere else and you miss your flight and are delayed in the airport for hours, there's a reason for that, too. There is work to be done there—maybe in the form of a life-changing conversation or perhaps a more subtle, yet equally important, experience. Take comfort in knowing that whatever eventually happens in your life, or your community, or the world, that is exactly what is supposed to happen.

There is no point in resisting your location or situation. Trying to control it will lead to nothing but frustration. Just open yourself up to seeing what the Creator is showing you! If you can, you'll send me packing. Just like that.

You know the story about the man who is hanging from a cliff in a snowstorm? He begs God for help. God says, "Just let go, and I'll catch you." I'm listening in, so I say to the man, "What are you, nuts? You'll die." The man hangs on and the next morning, they find the poor guy frozen to death, still clinging to the cliff, just three feet from the ground.

I win by talking you into bad choices. You win by letting go—letting go of what you think is good for you, that is. That's because when you do that, you get more than you ever thought was possible. And I sure the heck don't live in the realm of possibility. That's God's domain.

CHAPTER TWELVE:
TEST NUMBER THREE
CAN YOU LEARN TO WAIT (FOR THE RIGHT MOMENT)?

When you plant a seed in the ground, does it instantaneously bear fruit? Of course not. You wouldn't expect it to, either. All things that bear fruit stay hidden for a time. This is a Universal Truth in both the physical and spiritual worlds. It's called *Concealment*, and who better to tell you about all things hidden than yours truly?

You see, if you allow time for the process of Concealment, you ensure that great things will be unleashed into the world. Hurry the process along, on the other hand, and you'll have nothing but a dormant seed with no sprout in sight. Does that sound anything like death to you? It sure does to me.

So, what does my little seed metaphor mean to you? It means that before your greatness can be revealed, your patience will be tested. And not just your patience, either. I'll test your ego—that need to be out there and important right now. Here's a tip, by way of preparation. When the moment of decision comes, you'll hear a voice inside you saying, "Why wait when you can have it all now?"

Any guesses as to whose voice that would be?

DIVINE INCUBATION

There is a period in every person's life when you know that you are capable of so much more than you are doing, and the desire to burst into action is practically palpable. But remember this: All great work—no matter if it is a spiritual, business, or intellectual endeavor—requires an incubation period.

In other words, you can't just want it; you've got to wait for it. Take the company Microsoft, for instance. It didn't become a multinational company in a day. Bill Gates operated in relative obscurity for years before his company gained the success it enjoys today. It's the smart folks—the ones who I haven't gotten a firm grip on yet—who recognize that they could offer even more to the world if they stepped out of its line of sight for a time to reflect and mature. It is only with a consciousness of humility and openness that a person can understand the nature of Concealment. That's because if you lack the desire to wait and see what the Light really has in store, then I've still got you. In fact, I'm at my absolute best when I work with people who have an addiction to the spotlight, a lack of patience, and a need for recognition.

The greatest example of concealment I can give you involves a Kabbalist by the name of Rav Shimon bar Yochai. This was a man untouchable by me, a man fully plugged in to the Light.

RAV SHIMON BAR YOCHAI

Rav Shimon lived in Israel in the second century, a very turbulent time of Roman rule. Rav Shimon took up residence in a secluded cave in the mountains. Many believed that he was trying to escape persecution from the Romans, but this doesn't make much sense because Rav Shimon was the most powerful man who ever walked this Earth. He was one of only a handful of men to call me out, to challenge me, and win. His presence in this world created so much Light that there could be no free will; when you were in his presence, you couldn't possibly make a negative choice!

Rav Shimon put himself in a state of Concealment so that he could do the best possible work on your behalf. Truth be told, he did not want to repeat Moses' mistake of leaving part of the work to other people who might mess up. It was during Rav Shimon's time in the cave that he revealed the *Zohar*, the greatest weapon ever to be used in the fight against me. The *Zohar* contains all the wisdom of the universe, along with the Hidden Light that can ultimately remove me from this dimension.

You can imagine how I tried to stop it. All the while, this man exhibited extraordinary patience. He understood the process completely. Here he had the most powerful gift humanity had ever seen, but he kept it under wraps, not only in his own lifetime but for the generations that followed. It took 1200 years before his great work became known to humanity.

What is the truth behind Concealment? When you are concealed and not boasting about your greatness, when you are hidden away from the outside world, what you are really hidden from is me. This is the only way your seed can grow and blossom without my influence.

For 13 years, Rav Shimon lived with his son, Rav Elazar, in a cave in complete isolation while the greatest wisdom of the universe was being revealed to him. His willingness to go into hiding and to suppress his body's needs and comforts is what earned him the permission to receive this knowledge, and to serve as the channel for bringing it to the world.

MY TACTICS

In order to dissuade you from the benefits of Concealment, I'll plant the following thoughts in your mind:

- Patience will get me nowhere.
- I have to make things happen now.
- Why is it that no one recognizes all that I'm doing, and how great I am?

To pass the test of Concealment, you must learn to override these thoughts and become content with not being known, as well as not knowing when the right time will come. You have to tune out my voice, which says, "It's now or never!"

Consider the birth of a child. Surely, there is no other time in your life when you are more like the Creator. And yet, it takes nine months, from concealment to revelation, before the miracle of life is complete.

Bottom line: There is a time and a place for everything, and only God can determine it. But I will do everything I can to convince you that it's up to you (me) to make the call. And if you're out there listening to me, I will either make you come out before it's time or I will make you stay in hiding, which is very different from Concealment. When you hide, I have full reign.

CHAPTER THIRTEEN:
TEST NUMBER FOUR
CAN YOU MANAGE GOD'S MONEY? OR SHOULD I DO IT FOR YOU?

People consistently misunderstand one thing in this physical world more than anything else. That thing is money—booty, bread, lettuce.... You know what I'm talking about. The trick is that money has both physical and spiritual aspects, which is why most people don't know how to handle it. Here's how you can tell that money is not a strictly physical entity: Is the paper that it's printed on what you crave, or is it the way money makes you feel?

I thought so.

I come into play by either making you believe that you are entitled to it or, on the flip side, by leading you to believe that you don't deserve it. With a little help from me, most people react to monetary issues in ways they would never react to other aspects of their lives. If you want to see some really selfish behavior, stir money into the mix and see what happens.

If you have money, you're almost guaranteed to abuse the power it gives you. And if you don't have money, you are probably consumed by the lack of it. Is there a friend you wouldn't betray if tens of millions of dollars were on the line? Take a look at divorce: People will practically run their children over for money, or at least leave them badly hurting. People will kill over money. The only greater cause of murder is religion, and money isn't far behind.

To have a balanced relationship with money, you need to respect its energy. And just as you fail to understand God's power, you don't understand the invisible nature of the power of money, or how to manage it. In fact, your relationship with money is a reflection of your relationship with the Creator. Like the Light of the

Creator, you have to earn money to keep it. Sure, I'll give you little hits of it here and there to keep you addicted to me, but the real endless sustenance you are meant to have is something that must be earned. And you can't earn it until you can appreciate it, rather than waste or hoard it.

TWO FRIENDS

There once were two friends, Sam and Joe. They grew up together, got married at the same time, had kids at the same time, and grew their businesses a few blocks away from each other, until one day Sam had to move away.

Over the years, both friends became extremely wealthy. After several years, a bad business decision brought Sam to the edge of financial collapse. He did not know what else to do, so he decided to ask his old friend, Joe, for some help. He went back to his old town and knocked on Joe's door. Joe answered. Sam stood there and told Joe his story. Joe said, "Come in, my dearest and most beloved friend. Of course I will help. I will take half of my worldly wealth and give it to you."

Gotta love this guy, right?

Sam took the money and rebuilt his business; this time his empire grew even bigger. In fact, he became one of the wealthiest men in the country. However, fortune was not so kind to Joe. He lost everything, not long after he had given his money to Sam. But Joe was sure that Sam might be willing to help him out as he had once helped Sam.

When the two men met and Joe asked for help, Sam said, "I wish I could help you. It's just that all my money is tied up in investments right now. I'm sorry, Joe." Joe told Sam that he understood and went back home.

Joe died a poor man. But thanks to his generosity and unconditionally loving heart, the angels came and took Joe to those otherworldly Dimensions I mentioned earlier. One day, he witnessed a surprising scene. Joe saw me tormenting a selfish soul who had been greedy all his life. Joe looked closer and recognized the soul as his good friend, Sam. He begged the Creator to give Sam another chance. Because of Joe's greatness and his compassion for his friend, the Creator agreed, but I was able to step in and see to it that Sam would be given an exceedingly important test.

Both Sam and Joe came back to this world in new bodies. Sam became a wealthy miser who lived on a hill and shared with no one. Joe became a homeless person whose bones were fragile from malnutrition. One day, Joe climbed the stairs to the wealthy Sam's house and knocked on the door. Sam opened the door and Joe begged, "Please, sir, can you give me some money for food?"

"Are you crazy?" Sam said, "Don't you know that I never give money to anyone? Get off my property, you crazy beggar, before I shoot you myself!" Joe pleaded and begged, but it didn't matter; I had such a strong hold on Sam that no Light could penetrate. Sam took out his shotgun and, with barely a hint of hesitation, shot the ragged homeless man. Sam had removed a menace from society, I led him to believe, and his sense of righteousness was enough to darken the entire town. Little did Sam know that it was Joe—his friend from a previous lifetime—who was fighting to give him his last opportunity, and that he had failed the test miserably.

So, you see, sometimes when a person is born into wealth, it is not because they are good and deserving, but because they owe much, and are being tested. This man, Sam, had dug himself into a pretty deep hole, with some help from me. And that is where he chose to stay, amid my darkness.

So, listen up. This is important. The money you get in this world is not yours; it is energy that you were given to manage, as a custodian. It is a tool that can either help you in doing what you came to this world to do or hurt you. If you have too much money, you can become a slave to it, instead of letting it be a source of giving. Your lesson, in that case, is to override your greed and give. If you have too little, you might lose your connection with the Creator because you're struggling so hard just to put food on the table. Your lesson in this case might be to trust that God will fill in the blanks. You never know exactly how the Creator will help to take you to the next level. But you can predict—with certainty—that the Creator will, every time. Who knows which opportunity will lead to the money you need to pay your rent?

You will run up against tests that challenge your relationship with money and God. That's a sure thing. And you can't afford to mess this up. An eternity in paradise is on the line here, folks. This is your wake-up call.

Oh, and just in case you were wondering, souls do return to this physical world over and over until they finally get it right. Some people call this reincarnation. Whatever you call it, the wheel of life never stops turning. A soul never dies; it only changes form according to what it has left to do. And trust me, God will always provide you with every opportunity necessary for you to complete your work. God's good that way. So, that might mean great wealth for you or it might mean poverty. You have the ability to change your destiny either way. That's the point.

CHAPTER FOURTEEN:
TEST NUMBER FIVE
ARE YOU WILLING TO FIGHT FOR YOUR SOUL MATE...OR HAVE YOU GIVEN UP ALREADY?

SEPARATED AT BIRTH

You were separated from your soul mate in the very beginning, which means that a critical part of your spiritual work here on Earth is to rediscover one another. Bad dates, missed opportunities, unhealthy relationships that's where I come into play. My goal is to wear you down, so you'll give up. That's the test: Will you give up or keep searching? If you want to pass this doozie, you had best keep your eyes on the prize.

EXCUSES, EXCUSES

Let's say you're 29 years old, doing well at work, and focused on moving up the corporate ladder. Sure, you go on dates from time to time, but I've convinced you that finding love should not be high on your priority list. Your career is far more important.

But I'm lying to you.

At the level of your soul, you cannot do your *real* work without your soul mate. No matter how successful you are in your career, it will not last and it will never completely fulfill you. And I'm not talking about the need to have a family. Age is irrelevant in the soul mate search. Even if you are 100 years old and still single, keep working on your desire. Keep searching to find your matching half. No matter what excuses or lies I feed you, you can't throw in the towel. This test is too important.

Sound challenging? Of course it is—for those who are single, as well as for those who are with someone who's not the right one.

If you're stuck in a relationship, are you staying because of fear? If it's out of fear, or loneliness, then I've gotten the best of you. I've kept you blissfully unaware that things can be different—and not just different, but truly fulfilling. Your soul mate is probably standing right in front of your eyes, but you can't see this person; you have remained oblivious until this moment. Now you want to know more. Finally. Good for you.

It's time for you to feel entitled to a soul mate. It's time to fight for what belongs to you. The only reason you are in this situation is because you don't know that you can expect true happiness; finding your soul mate is a part of your destiny! In paradise, no one is alone. This absolute knowing—this consciousness of entitlement—is the Vessel for desire. It's absolutely essential.

If you fall into my trap, and choose to believe you are one of the few people to whom the Laws of the Universe do not apply, you will give up on your desire. But if you know it is coming to you—that the universe literally owes it to you—then you will not give up until you get what you deserve. You will turn over every stone. Check around every corner. You will do whatever it takes. Even if I am standing in your way—where I am guaranteed to be.

THE YOUNG SCHOLAR

There was a young scholar who would later become a great wise man and adversary of mine. He would get up at three o'clock every morning to study, overcoming his desire to sleep to overcome the control I had over his body (this is one of the tactics the great kabbalists used to elude my grasp). Every night, his wife would prepare a cup of tea for his study. But after several years, his wife needed to leave this world, so his mother stepped in and prepared his tea. One time, his mother was not able to make the tea, so she asked the neighbor to please have her daughter prepare it. They agreed.

The neighbor's daughter prepared the tea and snacks, delivering it to the scholar, who was so absorbed in his studies that he didn't even look up. Later that morning, the young scholar asked his mother if she had prepared his tea this time. "No," she replied, "It was the neighbor's daughter who prepared your tea. Why do you ask? Was everything OK?"

The scholar replied, "Yes, everything was fine. But in all the time my wife was alive, she prepared only one cup of tea. And all these years, you have prepared only one cup of tea. This woman, however, prepared two cups of tea."

When he saw that his mother could offer no explanation, the kabbalist went to the neighbor's daughter and said, "Can I ask you just one question? Why did you prepare two cups of tea?" She responded, "Well, you were studying with someone, so I decided to make two cups."

The scholar was amazed. He told her, "In all these years, neither my mother nor my first wife knew that I was studying with Elijah, the Prophet. But you did." At that moment, he knew he had found his soul mate. It was then that he asked for her hand in marriage.

From my point of view, this story demonstrates a clear failure on my part. If I had been on my game, these two would never have met. But this shows how God works if you let the Light in. God places people in your life at the right time, if you are willing to be open to the Light, open to the possibility, open to what God has in store. The young scholar knew almost immediately that it was the Creator who put this young woman in his life. He was plugged in to the Light, and so was she. I didn't have much hope of stepping into the picture.

And that's how it can work if you leave a little space every day for your soul mate's energy to find you. Are you willing to fight for what belongs to you? If you are, it's time to stake your claim.

CHAPTER FIFTEEN:
TEST NUMBER SIX

ARE YOU WILLING TO GO ALL THE WAY? (GIVING OVER OF THE SOUL/ *MESIRUT NEFESH*)

Now, remember that I gave you fair warning. The tests keep on coming, and this one can be a real kick in the pants. It requires that you completely surrender your soul. That sounds like something I would ask you to do, right? Give your soul to me. But this is not that at all, actually. Nor is it some sort of a religious ritual. This is about you getting your life back. It's a classic paradox. You let go completely, and get total control in return.

In order to defeat me and become my master—instead of the other way around—you must be willing to go all-out for something. I know that you're used to serving me. You'd do anything to save your ego, right? But now you need to be willing to do anything to save you—the *real* you. To become a master, you need to become a servant, because when you are operating with the consciousness of a servant, then everything the universe dishes out becomes an opportunity. That way, I have no pull, no influence, over any of your thoughts or actions. Servant consciousness is the polar opposite of victim consciousness. It's total surrender.

Victims resist whatever happens and feel that they are being done to. Someone who surrenders says, "You know what? There is something for me to do here. Let's see what I can find." Appreciating every opportunity is the path to fulfillment. Sure, I will try to convince you that life sucks and that God is out to get you, but when you transform your consciousness and don't listen to me, you take back control.

But like the rest of my advice to you, it's easier in theory than in practice. That's the whole point, isn't it? Without these tests, there is no growth. When things don't go your way—when pain, disease, or frustration enter the picture—you have a choice between stagnancy or growth. You can:

1. Choose to be a victim, or
2. Choose to surrender to the process.

Go ahead and scream out in frustration, "God, why are you doing this to me?" Then I've got you. I've got you operating in victim consciousness. Perfect. Servant consciousness, on the other hand, means performing the necessary spiritual work *in spite of the difficulty you are facing*. You do this knowing that the Creator is there, even when it seems like God has hung you out to dry. You get through this challenge by knowing you don't have the perspective that the Creator has. You do this in spite of me.

I've seen it happen from time to time. You have said *no* to playing the role of the victim. You didn't succumb to my influence. However, you didn't surrender to the Creator, either. You existed in limbo, purgatory—a state of only partial surrender. You wanted to have your cake and eat it, too. But this state offers you little in the way of fulfillment or control. It isn't until you completely let go of victimhood and enter true surrender that you win.

If you truly recognized that you don't get anything you can't handle, surrender would come easier. Even the worst scenarios—disease, death, and destruction—can be turned into Light. But most of the time, you don't believe that.

If you can learn to completely let go of everything and take total responsibility, you can reach another level. Yes, there is another level beyond surrendering, and that is Becoming Like God.

BECOMING LIKE GOD

Becoming like God is a longing—a yearning—that you'vc got to possess. It is knowing that the challenges of this world are temporary, and that the best is yet to come. Pretend that you are living in a small room with little sunlight and no one with whom to talk. What would you do? What would be your first step in getting out of this situation?

Easy. Your first step would be to develop a longing for something more, something far better than the cramped, dank room that you find yourself in. Likewise, you must have a hunger for something far greater than your current, measly existence. Your life is like the tiny room that I described—in fact, it's the tiny room that I have tried to keep you in for a long, long time. To do so, I have kept the infinitely spacious and sun-filled playground that was designed for you hidden. You must long for this place, in the same way God longs to fill your Vessel with Light. You must nurture and develop this yearning until it is all that you are. This is your first step in becoming like God. The next step on the road to becoming like God is understanding that everything belongs to God. Nothing belongs to you—not your gifts, your talents, your material possessions, not even your children.

***Everything* is borrowed.**

As much as the Creator adores you, the Creator also has no

emotional attachment to your thoughts or behaviors. Can you imagine what it means to love without end and without condition, while simultaneously feeling no attachment to the physical components which make up the material world? This is what being like God means.

Becoming like God also demands that you see the Light behind everything. Do you see a system behind the trees, the animals, and all of nature? Do you see God all around you? If I am doing my job, most of the time you probably don't. But if you can wake up and start seeing God in absolutely everything—even in situations that seem "bad" or unfortunate—then I have no hold on you whatsoever.

How are you when it comes to seeing opportunity? The life you are leading now is a profoundly unique opportunity, which won't come around in exactly the same way ever again. Your existence as it is right now is your best shot to do the job you arrived here to do; you don't know how your "next time" will look. Every day, every hour, every moment, is an opportunity.

And God never misses a beat. He sees every situation as a chance for spiritual expansion, an opportunity to share more Light with the universe. This is the consciousness that you, too, must bring to the Game if you are to be in perfect alignment with the Creator.

The only thing that is truly yours is your use of time. Time is the currency of life. Every moment counts, which means that how you choose to spend your time determines everything. God fully spends His time in share mode. If you are not doing the same, then you can't become like God. I can't make this any clearer. If you spend your moments sharing, you are behaving just like the Creator; anything else falls short of the goal.

I cause you to sink into feelings of guilt, hopelessness, helplessness, and defeat much of the time—emotions the Light of the Creator doesn't even recognize. You are still letting me in, still letting me convince you that what you have done is written in stone, unchangeable, and that you should repent for your mistakes until the end of time.

But it's that type of thinking that leads to not admitting your mistakes and, therefore, failing to make the necessary corrections. The moment you admit your mistakes, you allow the Light into the situation. And with the Light, everything—absolutely everything—is fixable. No matter how low I have caused you to go, you have the power to turn it around. Completely.

Joseph hit bottom. He was seduced by the wife of another man—to the point where he was naked before her—yet, in the end, he still chose the path of the Light and refused her. This was one of my more remarkable defeats, I might add. A man who was so close to darkness yet was still able to amend the situation is truly God-like. Instead of saying, "I've gone this far; why not finish what I have started?" he restricted his self-satisfying behavior, and became one with God.

To know that there is always a way out in any moment of darkness is to align with the Nature of God. To become like God, you must see the impermanence of all situations, and the inherent "fixability" that inhabits every moment.

ISAAC AND ABRAHAM

Maybe you know this one. It's a Bible story that gets told a lot, so I bet you do. It's the one about Abraham and his son, Isaac. As the story goes, God made a request of Abraham that he sacrifice Isaac. Despite the enormity of the request, Abraham didn't fall into victim mode; instead, he prepared to sacrifice his only son. Isaac was bound to the altar for sacrifice, but, at the last minute, Isaac's life was spared.

This story is a metaphorical blueprint for defeating me. Abraham represents a perfect force of giving and sharing. Isaac represents a perfect force of receiving. Did you know that at the time of the binding, Abraham was 137 years old and Isaac was 37? You think a 37-year-old man is going to let his ancient dad cut his throat? Of course not. This story is just a way for God to relay a message without having to spell it out word for word. If God told you outright, you wouldn't have the chance to earn it for yourself. But I'm spelling it out for you right now: To beat me, you need the force of sharing to bind with the force of receiving.

Abraham's degree of willingness demonstrates his complete trust in the Creator's vision for his life. At this level of surrender, there is no separation between the Creator and his servant. At this level, you Becoming Like God.

THE FOUR LEVELS OF DESIRE

There's another vital piece of the puzzle here. And that puzzle piece is desire. When a person desires something, he or she will do one of four things:

1. Try to make it happen.
2. Do everything he or she can to make it happen.
3. Make it happen, no matter what.
4. Make it happen, but for someone else.

These are the four levels of desire, and depending on your level of desire, you'll experience different results. If your desire is great, you won't rest until you make it happen, right? Period. End of story. You just get the job done. But if you choose to listen to my doubts, you'll give it a go, but eventually you'll throw in the proverbial towel, after convincing yourself that you've done everything you could.

And for the person who has the type of desire that makes him do something strictly for the sake of another—this person is master of the universe. To put it simply, the person who makes it happen, but for someone else, is becoming Like God.

Here's a word for those with that highest degree of desire: You will be tested, even harder than the rest. You will be asked to forfeit that one thing for which you've worked your whole life. For what *seems* like no reason, you'll be asked to give it up to make someone else's dream come true. This is the stuff of great movies, right? It's also the stuff of a great reality.

Are you prepared? Are you prepared to do anything, any way, any how, to make it happen, to become like God, and put me to rest forever? It's big stuff, isn't it? I bet you're starting to feel the burden of your task. Don't worry—defeating me might be the fight of your lifetime, but you don't have to do it all by yourself.

In fact, in order to carry out God's requests, you need someone on your side, someone who's got your back, so to speak. It starts with a friend or a spouse, a person you can count on, no matter what. Having this type of relationship in your life is the ultimate weapon against me. I cease to have any influence at all when I'm faced with a partnership of this magnitude.

THE APPLE THIEF AND THE SHOPKEEPER

There once was a king who ruled his kingdom with an iron fist. And he had good reason. The vast number of his subjects were fully and utterly corrupt. They were ruthless scoundrels who were only out to save their own hides.

One day, a man by the name of Nathaniel was caught stealing an apple. Nathaniel was not really a bad person (none of you are), and it wasn't his nature to steal from anyone. But after living among so many villains for so many years, he simply gave in to me, his selfish instinct, on this one occasion. Unfortunately, it was a bad time to make a mistake.

The king decided to make an example of Nathaniel in order to send a message to the rest of the people. The king sentenced Nathaniel to death. Nathaniel accepted his fate without any fuss. After all, he had no one to blame but himself. No victim consciousness here.

When the king asked Nathaniel if he had any last request, it turned out that he did. Nathaniel asked if he could have three days to settle various affairs in his life. Nathaniel had to pay off some debts, he owed a few personal favors, and he wanted to say good-bye to all of his loved ones. He figured he could tidy it all up in three days.

The king, impressed by Nathaniel's simple acceptance of his fate and by his sense of responsibility, wanted to accommodate this last request. But there was an obvious problem. "If I grant you this temporary reprieve," the king said, "I have no assurances that you will ever return to fulfill your sentence."

Nathaniel understood the king's dilemma. "I have an idea," Nathaniel responded. "Suppose I arrange for a good friend to stand in for me until I return. If I am late, you can execute my friend in my place." The king laughed. "If you can find someone who will take your place, I will grant you your three days. But if you are even one minute late, you can be sure your friend will be hung from the gallows."

Nathaniel asked his best friend, a shopkeeper by the name of Simon, to stand in his place. Simon had known Nathaniel since they were young children. He loved him like a brother and respected his friend dearly. Simon said he would be honored to go into temporary custody for Nathaniel.

Simon was handcuffed and detained while Nathaniel hurried off to wind up his affairs. "Remember," the king yelled out, "One minute late and I will hang your best friend."

One day passed, and then two more and still Nathaniel did not return. The king ordered Simon to the gallows and the hangman's noose was slipped around Simon's neck. The hangman tightened it, and a hood was put over Simon's head.

Just then, a voice was heard screaming far off in the distance. "Stop! Stop! I have returned!" It was Nathaniel. "Please, I beg you," Nathaniel cried to the king. "Remove the noose. This is my fate, not his."

But the king replied, "You are an hour late."

Nathaniel was so out of breath he could hardly talk. "Let me explain, your majesty. My horse became lame. I was forced to run all the way back. That is why I am late. It is I who should die. Not my dear friend."

As the hangman removed the hood from Simon's head, Simon began to shout himself. "That is not true. I am the one who should die today. We had an agreement. Besides, I could not stand here and watch you, my best friend, die before my eyes. Nor could I bear living without you. You were late. So, it will be I who will die today."

Nathaniel's eyes welled up with tears. "I beg you, your majesty. Do not listen to him. Do not let my best friend die. I could no more live without him than he could live without me. It is I who was originally sentenced to death, not Simon. I beg you to get on with my execution." As Simon and Nathaniel continued arguing back and forth, the king was, not surprisingly, taken aback. In a land rampant with hooligans, the king was not accustomed to seeing such acts of generosity and unconditional friendship. Nevertheless, a decision had to be made. Justice had to be meted out according to the law of the land.

"I have reached a final verdict," the king said. "Neither one of you shall die. For I realize that no matter which one of you dies today, I will still be killing two men. The original sentence called for only one man to die. Thus, I am forced to set you both free."

Talk about an example of an unshakable friendship, of complete surrender, of doing whatever it takes.... Of zero victim consciousness! There was not a trace of self-interest within the hearts of these two men. They were untouchable! They considered only the welfare of the other, unconditionally, with no strings attached. Both men took full responsibility for their circumstances and were willing to make the ultimate sacrifice for each other. By doing so, the two men became as one and were able to remove death from both of their lives. By the way, the king asked to be their friend.

So, by taking full responsibility, by being present with your circumstances, and by being completely there for another person, you become immortal! This makes you one with God, in which case my favorite tool, the ego, no longer has power over you. When you give 100 percent to another person, two literally become one, and there is no longer room for me to work my dark brand of magic.

CHAPTER SIXTEEN:
TEST NUMBER SEVEN
CAN YOU KEEP THE PEACE (WITH ME BREATHING DOWN YOUR NECK)?

I like to stir the pot. That's how I operate. When I am the chef, you can bet that the kitchen will get hot. If you leave me to call the shots, you know that I'll be injecting my special recipe of jealousy, judgment, and envy. But I won't stop there. I'm even more effective if I can cause you to sabotage and judge yourself in the same way! So, the test for you is to stop me before I start stirring up trouble.

If you think you are up to the challenge, you'll definitely need some tools. Ever heard of a truth serum? When a person swallows it, he or she becomes powerless to hold back the truth. Your first tool is to seek this serum. If you want to oust me, you have to become a die-hard truth-seeker. Rav Ashlag—one of my toughest adversaries, I might add—was just such a man.

Rav Ashlag was a 20th century Kabbalist—someone who learned to recognize the illusions of the material world, and the truth beneath my ploys. Revealing the truth starts with asking questions, and that is precisely what Rav Ashlag did. For every one answer he received, he asked 15 more questions. The truth was paramount for him, as it should be for you.

But most people find it a lot easier to judge than to search for the truth. Passing judgment on others doesn't seem nearly as scary as discovering what is really going on beneath the surface. But if your goal is a life of joy and fulfillment, the path starts with discovering the truth. This means being honest with others and yourself. It also means that you've got to learn to put a muzzle on me!

The next step requires a shift in consciousness, moving from self-interest to having the best intentions for others in your heart. When you intend the best for others, you are bringing Light into the lives of others.

Aaron, Moses' brother, was a champ at this. As hard as I would work to undo people's most cherished relationships, he would build bridges between the two souls in conflict. We're talking about a man who would seek out troubled relationships in order to bring the two people together again. He was a schemer, but one like no other. He was the master of conflict resolution before the term was ever coined. This was a man who always knew the right way to turn darkness into Light.

HUSBAND AND WIFE

Let's look at the sacred peace between a husband and a wife. Because this relationship is vital to the flow of Light in the universe, its peace should never be shattered by another. I might tempt you in any number of ways, but when you allow me to break the peace of your marriage, you are opening the floodgates to darkness in your life and in the lives of others.

God's a pro at keeping the peace. Take, for instance, the time, in the Bible story, when the angels delivered the news to Sarah that she'd be having a child. She laughed out loud, commenting on her husband Abraham and how he was too old to give her a child. Ever the diplomat, God did not reveal this tidbit to Abraham when speaking with him later. God simply said that Sarah had made it clear that she wasn't able to have children. The Creator understood that Sarah's comment might hurt Abraham's feelings and cause a rift between husband and wife, so the Creator just edited it out.

GOING TO WAR FOR PEACE

The final step of your peace mission might sound like pure paradox, but, as we've seen, such is the nature of the universe. You need to be willing to go to war to achieve peace. Now, as much as I like to see hand to hand combat, I'm not talking about a physical war between soldiers—I'm talking about the war within. You must be willing to fight to the death against me, and every negative emotion I elicit. Consider a man who knows that his marriage is on the rocks. He must be willing to fight for his marriage, to bring every ounce of Light he can into the marriage, in order to save it. This is what I mean by being willing to go to war for peace.

So, the sooner you come to terms with the fact that this is indeed a battle to the death, the sooner I can exit stage right. Are you willing to go to war and confront all the demons that I bring to the table in order to find lasting, abiding peace—for yourself and for the rest of the world? Think long and hard about this answer, because your entire future hangs in the balance.

CHAPTER SEVENTEEN:
TEST NUMBER EIGHT
CAN YOU KEEP THE LIGHT OF DESIRE BURNING (NO MATTER WHAT)?

DESIRING THE "IMPOSSIBLE"

Let's get one thing straight: It's my mission to obliterate your desire, while it should be your greatest mission to keep your desire strong, healthy, and growing. What's the big deal with desire? Desire is essential to the fulfillment of your Vessel, and therefore of your dreams.

Now, this is not about letting go and surrendering the outcome to God. Desire is never something to be surrendered! It is the crucial component of your very relationship with God. And one key to maintaining desire is making sure that I don't wiggle my way in between you and God. You always need to be on the lookout for me, since, as you know by now, I can be tricky to spot. But if you start to believe that it is time to give up on your dreams, you can bet that I have definitely entered the Game.

Take, for instance, a 40-year-old woman who would like to have a child, but feels that it is too late. If she allows me to enter the picture, I'll convince her to throw in the towel straight away. But that is the test, you see, and it's a life-changing one. She must decide between succumbing to my doubts, or believing that anything under the sun can and will happen if you want it bad enough.

What would you do?

I'll tell you what I would do. To convince her to give up, I'd play the statistics card. It rarely fails when I am working with someone into whom I have already injected a bit of doubt. Having children after the age of 40 is a gamble at best, I'd tell her. But I'll let you in on the truth. You shouldn't always listen to statistics—here's why:

Having children is as much a miracle at 20 as it is at 70! Regardless of age, conceiving a child requires Divine Intervention. The reason it doesn't often happen later in life is that people don't believe it can.

Think about it: God could create an evolutionary process in which it's normal for women to continue to menstruate until they are 100 years old. Most people don't believe that would be possible, but anything is possible when you're talking about the power of the Creator.

Look at history if you need proof. Travel by air seemed impossible at one time, but now we have a space shuttle that travels through the sky at 17,000 miles per hour. Our ancestors could only expect to live to age 40, under the best of circumstances. Now, you are capable of living twice as long as that, if not longer.

What guides the evolutionary process is what you believe to be possible. And that includes technology. Twenty years ago, leukemia was a death sentence. Not so today. If someone developed clogged arteries or heart disease, they were mine for the taking. Enter bypass surgery in the sixties.

Humans have the power to change, as does technology, which is spurred by human thought and innovation. So, why couldn't a woman develop the capability to have children at any age? What could possibly prevent technology from advancing to that point? The answer lies in your certainty. The scientist who will discover a cure for an "incurable" disease is the scientist who believes the cure is there to be found. Just as the woman who conceives at age 60 is the woman who knew it was possible. When it comes to spiritual transformation, you can throw statistics out the window. Consider a person who loses his home to a flood or fire. He might go through life thinking that:

A. He is less likely to lose his home again, so he shouldn't worry, or
B. If it happened once, why wouldn't it happen again?

Which way of thinking is right? Neither, because the tests you face in life aren't left up to chance. You are tested whenever it's necessary to move you to the next level toward perfection. You are tested when it's time to let go of the garbage you've been hauling around.

THE *P* WORD

What can you do to give over your disbelief? How can you transform the impossible into the possible? One word. *Prayer*. There, I said it. Part of making impossible things happen is prayer. If you want to defeat doubt—if you want to defeat me—start with prayer. Prayer lets Light in and forces me out. Prayer will make the difference, and it starts with knowing that it is your right—your duty even—to ask for the impossible.

That's what Hannah did. Do you know her story from the Bible? She did it without ever giving me the opportunity to stop her.

HANNAH'S PRAYER

Hannah was childless. Despite wanting children badly, she didn't succumb to my usual tactics. She resisted self-pity and would simply not give up hope that one day she would have a child. I watched her as she went to the Temple to pray. Hannah was so intent in her prayer—and so intent on her connection with the Creator—that she was actually swaying from side to side and mumbling beneath her breath as she prayed.

The people who prayed around her thought she was just an old drunk, but, being immune to me, she was also immune to their judgment; she heard not one of their negative comments, so lost was she in her connection. And her commitment paid off. She gave birth to the Prophet Samuel.

Like Hannah, it's time to start believing in and asking for the impossible. As it is with finding your soul mate, you are entitled to the "impossible" because you are entitled to all things good. So why not do what it takes to bring the impossible into this world? Perhaps having children is not a test or a challenge for you, but I know firsthand that you are facing other challenges that require you to stretch yourself beyond your current belief system. That's the space where you'll find God—outside of the limitations provided by me and by the material, finite world. There is no such thing as a fixed destiny.

When you feel like throwing in the towel, ask yourself: "What am I missing? Where is the goodness I am failing to see here?" I can guarantee that if you feel like giving up, you are missing the

Divine opportunity that stands before you. The Light is right before your eyes!

And if you keep taking the Light for granted, you'll lose it. That almost happened to Rav Nachum. He was a student under my nemesis, the Baal Shem Tov. He and I battled for a bit, as you'll see.

THE STUDENT AND THE THIEF

As a student of a wise teacher, Rav Nachum's job was to collect money for the poor. After spending days trying to collect money with no success, I finally had him on his knees. Rav Nachum was ready to quit. "Why do I have this job?" he cried out in frustration.

At that moment, a thief walked by. It was obvious to Rav Nachum that this thief was quite content, so he asked him why he was so happy. The thief replied, "I'm just doing my work. I came into this world to steal, and that's what I do. Maybe one day, I'll have the privilege to steal from you."

Rav Nachum reflected on the encounter. It was then that I could feel myself starting to lose my grip on him (when you start reflecting on your actions that tends to happen). I heard Rav Nachum say to himself, "I am a free man and the student of a great wise man, and I'm sad. He's a thief who will probably wind up in jail, and he's happy."

It was then that he got it. He saw what he had. The Light. The opportunity. Everything. And this reenergized him to fulfill his purpose, and he went above and beyond in his work of collecting money. When Rav Nachum returned to the Baal Shem Tov with the fruits of his labor and relayed the story of the happy thief who had inspired him to keep going, his teacher smiled.

Part of the consciousness around giving up is not realizing your gifts. In the moment you decide to give up, you cease appreciating all that you have been given. In the story, Rav Nachum had been given a gift in the form of a specific job and the skill to do it. A job doesn't get much better than that! Yet, he took this responsibility for granted, until the Creator sent him a sign and he met the thief who genuinely enjoyed the task *he* had been assigned.

The thief reawakened Rav Nachum's desire, and from that point forward, everything flowed as it should.

So what can you do to reignite your desire? You can pray for more.

Yes, you can ask the Creator for the ability to want more, to expect more, and to have more desire. In fact, you've got to—it is your obligation as a Vessel of Light to demand what is yours. You forget that the Creator is more than willing to work with you. The Creator will send you experiences and challenges to strengthen your resolve and nurture your desire. This is exactly why God asked me to give you all these tests. If you shut down your desire and refuse to ask for more, you're sending me an invitation that I won't turn down. But if you knew with certainty that an answer to your prayers was right around the corner, would you ever give up?

PRAYERS FOR MERCY

While I'm on the subject of prayer, I should mention a specific kind of prayer. A prayer for mercy. This is the strongest type of prayer you can offer up. Here's the deal. God will never leave you hanging—never. God will offer you the gift of mercy if you ask for it. If you have taken responsibility for your pain and suffering and have worked on healing it from the inside out, then it is your obligation to ask God to remove the burden. You ask this of God when the pain is too great to bear and if it is no longer helping you grow spiritually. God can and will step in to dissolve the pain for you if you are willing to ask for God's help.

By using this tool, you cease being a slave to pain—and to me. Instead, you rely on the Light of the Creator to heal you, just like a son or daughter relies on a loving parent. You are deserving of help; not only that, your birthright is a life free of suffering. Yes, I have worked hard to make you forget this little insignificant detail, but it is the truth. You are worthy of God's grace.

GOD WILL MEET YOU WHERE YOU ARE

Consider the story of a man that I "worked with" once. I had him swimming in debt up to his ears, miserable, and scared. He didn't see God in anything or anyone. I had him right where I wanted him. He owed so much money that his life was literally on the line. Needless to say, this was a very desperate man.

One day, he walked into his study and a book fell on his head. He picked up the book written by a wise man named Rav Nachman, and it fell open to a passage that simply said, "Don't give up."

Even I couldn't prevent him from heeding such a clear message from God! After reading the line, he chose to take on extra work, climbed out of the debt he was under, and turned his life around. Rav Nachman came to him in a dream that night and said, "When I wrote that in my book, I wrote that line for you."

Do you see how utterly simple the answer to the man's problem was? The guy just needed to keep moving forward. Thankfully, the Creator will meet you precisely where you are spiritually. If it takes a book falling on your head with the answer, then the Creator won't hesitate. There is always a solution in the Light!

I know that you've been right there, where the man in the story was. I know this because I was right there with you. You wanted to give up, maybe even take your own life. (Talk about the power of my influence!) It may have been during a midlife crisis, or right after you lost someone you loved. In your case, you managed to crawl out of that state of depression. I am impressed, and I know how you did it. You didn't give up because you continued to have some level of desire. You desired to live, to experience joy, and to find fulfillment. You desired these things because this is your nature; it's who you are.

DESIRE IT LIKE YOU'RE ADDICTED TO IT

I know you like shortcuts, so I know you'll like this one. You have to crave what you truly desire, just like a drug user craves a hit or like a sugar freak craves a piece of cake. (In those examples, the desire happens to be misplaced, but it's strong nonetheless.) It's not a question of whether or not you are going to get your fix (your fulfillment); it's only a matter of how. That is how strong your desire for Light should be. To realize your potential, you have to crave it with a passion. Anything less just won't cut it.

PART III:

THE END OF RELIGION

CHAPTER EIGHTEEN:

ABRAHAM'S LEGACY

Even if you pass all the tests I just prepared you for, I'll still be around if you haven't put an end to religion. I touched on this earlier, but please allow me the soapbox again. There are some details we need to discuss.

If you're really serious about finding paradise, here's what needs to happen. If the priests, rabbis, imams, and monks admitted their sins and all their followers acknowledged their sins, and you all ganged up on me (not each other)—if you finally figured out you were on the same team—it would be Game Over! If you were to stop pointing the finger at one another, I'd be toast. If you all did that, within five minutes, you'd see God's Light materializing right before your very eyes.

SALVATION WHERE YOU LEAST EXPECT IT

Obviously, I corrupt the religious establishment. And I corrupt all of you who follow any of the world's religions. You wind up blaming the establishment. The religious establishment winds up blaming other religions. And everyone runs around blaming each other. Meanwhile, I dine on all the gourmet delights you're feeding me.
I am going to take a few moments to directly address three special people who descend from Abraham, the Patriarch. I think this information is vital to your understanding of the bigger picture here.

Isaac.
Ishmael.
Esau.

Specifically, I will be addressing their offspring:

The Jews.
The Muslims.
The Christians.

The rest of you should not feel left out. You are equally important, and equally loved by the Creator. You are all one family. But these three siblings are the ones who are causing all the trouble in this dysfunctional family unit called humanity. It's time they cleaned it up.

I begin with the children of Ishmael.

THE MUSLIMS

Why do you think you bow five times a day? To thank *Allah*? To show respect and offer praise to *Allah*? Nope. *Allah* is all-powerful, all-loving, and omnipotent. He does not require thanks or praise. He doesn't want to receive. *Allah* just wants to share. And give. And love. The reason you bow five times a day is to ground your negativity, to bury your ego (me) in the very bowels of the earth. You need to bury me. That opens you up to receive the love of *Allah*.

You need to know that I am your only enemy. I am the only infidel. If you bow with the mind-set that your enemy is someone out there, I hijack all your prayers. If you meditate to bury your ego in the ground, your prayers will be magnified greatly.

Here's a tip. After bowing, as you rise back up, pray to raise your soul—the real you—into the Divine Realm so that you are constantly connected to *Allah*. Only I, the ego, your Adversary, prevent you from connecting yourself with *Allah*. No one else. When you bury me into the earth, five times a day, you will have the power to reach the Supernal Heavens with your consciousness.

THE CHRISTIANS

Jesus died for your sins. No question about it. But you have no idea what that means because I distorted everything about his story. Listen up: His death dealt me a great and powerful blow. But it wasn't a knockout punch. I am still here, aren't I? Look around. The world is worse than ever, isn't it? Do you really think God wanted to see you suffer all these centuries as you wait for the Final Apocalypse or a Second Coming? It was I who convinced you to do nothing but wait.

The generation of Israelites and pagans who lived during the time of Jesus was neck-deep in filth and self-indulgence. God intervened—by way of Moses—to bail out the Israelites 3400 years ago, and God was forced to intervene again 2000 years ago. Enter Jesus. Jesus took upon himself the task of eradicating my influence from this world. No one else had the guts to do so. He was ready to take on the entire religious establishment when he saw that I controlled them. But Jesus didn't blame them. Jesus knew he had to defeat me. Who am I? I am doubt. Doubt is the reason the whole religious establishment was corrupt in the first place.

Cut to Golgotha, the site of Jesus' crucifixion. Jesus is nailed to the cross. He's suffering. Then he cries out to God, asking why his Father has forsaken him. Do you know why he did that? He was expressing doubt. I am doubt. Jesus was challenging me. He was picking the fight of all fights. He wasn't expressing doubt about his Father. He was taunting me. He was summoning me.

The only way we defeat something is by facing it. So, when Jesus wanted to defeat me, he was forced to summon me. That is what took place at Golgotha. That is the secret behind the words of doubt he uttered.

Doubt was inside of him. I was inside of him. We were landing blows on each other. Then, a moment later, crucifixion. Jesus willingly sacrificed himself (his ego—me) while I was present in his consciousness. That was his best punch. And that action cleansed his generation and diminished my influence over the entire world enough to prevent its total annihilation.

Do you know why Golgotha is called *Golgotha*? It means "the place of the skull." Where do you think consciousness dwells? Where do you think the war is fought? Jesus fought the war against his own ego—me—inside his head. The death of his body was the death of me. In the place of the skull. In the place of human consciousness.

His actions saved the world. But only for a generation. Now, it's up to you. Jesus' teachings—his life, his ways—became the path for future generations to follow. You must walk that same path. You must wipe out *Satan*, your Adversary, by finding me within yourself. Inside the place of the skull—where that big brain of yours resides!

Don't listen to me. Listen to Jesus. Follow him. Accepting Jesus means accepting his teachings and his consciousness. If you get past me, if you get me out of that head of yours, you will see there is no contradiction in what you currently believe.

Would you be helping your children if you did all their homework for the rest of their lives? If you took all the punishments on their behalf every time they made a mistake or misbehaved? Would that be true parental love? Would your kids grow up to be responsible, loving adults if you absorbed all their punishments? This desire to help goes against the natural Law of the World. It is the opposite of love. It fails the test of unbalanced relationships. Parents are the full-time givers, remember?

Here's the truth. I will only say it once: What Jesus did for all Christians was offer a path to salvation. In his name and upon his merit, he cleared the path for you. But you still have to walk it. He suffered to open up the channels so that you could connect to the Hidden Dimensions and make contact with the Father. To do that, you need to defeat me. You were all given a chance to earn unimaginable rewards, but it requires finding and conquering me.

And the reason you never did find me within yourself, the reason you sat back and put it all on Jesus' shoulders, is because I told you to. Trust me on this. Your Savior is pissed off. He's angry with me for doing such a good job of deceiving you. But he's also upset with you for not taking me out of the Game yet.

And now I will offer a confession. It was his idea to write this book. To give you all a chance. Don't get me wrong. I wanted to write it, as well. I am cheering for you, even though I do my darndest to beat you. But it was his idea to send you this lifeline. Muhammad and Moses were in on it, too.

So, those of you who call yourself Christians, don't blame the Jews. Or the Church. Or the popes of history. Or devil-worshippers. Or the Church of Satan. Don't blame anyone, even if blame seems justified. It's a losing bet. Blame me. Only me. No one but me. Just know that I am your ego and not a horned demon spewing fire from my eyes and fingertips. Then put an end to me. And never forget—the only way to get to me is knowing I am your ego. No other way. Do that and it is Game Over. Don't do it and the fires keep burning.

THE ISRAELITES

You believe that when the Bible refers to Israelites, it's referring to Jews. But it's not. Israelites include Christians, Muslims, and Jews who see the good in everyone and see the unity in every tradition. An Israelite recognizes the holiness of Moses, of Jesus, and of Muhammad. An Israelite sees them as souls that came into this world to help you fight me. An Israelite is the opponent of jihad, of the right-wing Jewish extremist, and of any other crusader who only sees what's wrong with everyone else, or who wants to make everyone else accept his beliefs.

Israelites see no separation. They encompass everyone. They accept all others. Israelites allow people to be just as they are.

JIHAD, JEWISH EXTREMISTS, CRUSADERS

Let's talk about extremists, shall we?

There is only one holy war. One. Not two. It's the war against me. Your ego. Your enemy is the Great Satan. Not the people who occupy your land. Not the people who don't believe in your god. It's me. Only me. Yes, everyone in the world has a portion of me within them. But you cannot kill the force named *Satan* in another person. That's an exercise in futility.

You're hearing it straight from the horse's mouth. I am the one who motivates you to kill *Satan* in another person because I know it won't work. It never has, and it never will. Not only does it not work, it fortifies me. I grow stronger each time you try to take me out by taking out one of your fellow human beings. I trick you into believing you are in a war against each other. You're not. It's me you want. I am inside each one of you, coercing you into pointing the finger at everyone else.

So, Israelites are not Jews. That misconception, too, was my doing. Nowhere in the Bible does God mention creating a religion called Judaism. There is only the path of defeating me; the one who masters that path merits the designation *Israelite*.

CHAPTER NINETEEN:

YOUR ACE IN THE HOLE AGAINST RELIGION

THE ULTIMATE WEAPON

I read Latin. I understand Greek. I comprehend English. I'm conversant in Italian. Fluent in French. Articulate in Arabic. And I speak Hebrew. I totally get those languages. There's only one language I don't understand: Aramaic.

Jesus held his most private conversations in Aramaic for that very reason. He dished out hidden wisdom to his closest disciples using Aramaic. He employed the same language when he spun parables to the masses, parables that concealed the secrets of the universe (*Prisca Theologia*). There was nothing I could do. I couldn't eavesdrop on the disciples. I was unable to make head or tail out of the parables. Instead, I had to wait until the Aramaic teachings of Jesus were translated into other languages. Then, I set to work creating all the confusion that now surrounds religion.

Aramaic was a metaphysical tool from God to give you the ability to bypass my influence. That was one of the original Universal Rules set up to govern this reality.

I cannot interfere with prayers uttered in Aramaic. I can't touch them. But your prayers in other languages are no problem. I can interfere with roadblocks, detours, and stumbling blocks. (Remember, my name means *to block*). It's hard to sneak a prayer past me. And this is one of the reasons why your prayers often go unanswered. I interfere. I hear the prayers of the world all day and all night and I reroute them to nowhere.

But Aramaic? No dice. It's off-limits. It's untouchable. It's your direct connection to the Divine. It's broadband. It's superbroadband.

Aramaic was the predominant language during the time of the Prophet Muhammad in the seventh century. In fact, Aramaic was once as common as English is today. Aramaic is the root of Arabic. Mecca, the holiest city in Islam, is an Aramaic word (*Maccah*) that means "to break through." *Maccah* is also the name of one of the windows through which prayers must pass to reach the Divine Light. Put the two definitions together and you understand why Muslims direct their prayers toward Mecca. It is the window a prayer uses in order to reach the Realm of the Divine. Simple.

The ancient Israelites wrote secret books which revealed all the mysteries of the universe. These books were written in Aramaic so that I would not be able to read them. This includes sections of the Book of Daniel, and another secret book that I cannot and will not ever mention. This other book is my kryptonite. So, don't even bother asking.

So, now that Christians, Muslims, and Israelites had a common thread, I had to do something drastic. I had to cut the thread. I had to create conflict between the three faiths.

You see, Aramaic didn't belong to the Israelites. Or to the Christians. Or to the Muslims. It belonged to all of them—just like the Light of the sun belongs to all of them, irrespective of their particular beliefs. That was its secret. Aramaic is universal. It is the secret for unifying the three faiths. And prayers in Aramaic reach the Divine. That means that if enough Israelites, Christians, and Muslims put this power behind their prayers, it would undo me. Forever.

So you know what I did? I turned Aramaic into a dead language. I phased it out over the centuries. Then I buried it. I methodically severed Aramaic's connection to Arabic, and thereby to Muslims. Then, I cut it off from Jesus and Christians.

So, listen up Muslims, Christians, and Israelites—I will only explain this once. Arabic is Divine. Latin, Greek, and English are Divine. Hebrew is Divine. And so is Aramaic. Everything, including all languages spoken on Earth, originated from the one God.

But only Aramaic is off-limits to me. And that is its underlying power. It's not that Aramaic is holier than Arabic or Hebrew. It's just that Aramaic is beyond my reach.

Did you ever wonder why it's taking your prayers in your native language so long to change the world and transform your life? If you're a Muslim, did your Arabic prayers bring you world peace yet? No. The children of Ishmael are dying every day and your enemies still exist.

If you're a Christian, did your particular Latin, Greek, or English prayers bring you world peace yet? No. The disciples of Jesus Christ are still hurting, suffering, and dying every day.

If you're an Israelite, did your Hebrew prayers bring you world peace yet? No. You are still persecuted, complaining, and miserable after all these centuries.

How long before you wise up? It should boggle your mind: 2000 years of unanswered prayers and still you hope and wait!

You're now at a critical juncture in human history. My stranglehold has put you—all of humanity—into a collective coma. The Big Sleep. You are approaching total destruction. Consequently, for the first time in history, I am lending you a hand. I am interfering just to get you out of this mess. I will give you one advantage over me—but that's it. Be forewarned. After I give it to you, I will then use all my powers to persuade you not to employ this weapon. I have to. That's my job. If, however, you rise to the occasion and you take advantage of what I am about to give you, you'll be able to let me replace you in experiencing the pain that is to come.

You will all wind up living happily ever after.

THE 72 NAMES

Here it is: A sequence of Aramaic letters.

כהת	אכא	ללה	מהש	עלם	סיט	ילי	והו
הקם	הרי	מבה	יזל	ההע	לאו	אלד	הזי
חהו	מלה	ייי	נלך	פהל	לוו	כלי	לאו
ושר	לכב	אום	ריי	שאה	ירת	האא	נתה
ייז	רהע	חעם	אני	מנד	כוק	להח	יחו
מיה	עשל	ערי	סאל	ילה	וול	מיכ	ההה
פוי	מבה	נית	ננא	עמם	החש	דני	והו
מחי	ענו	יהה	ומב	מצר	הרח	ייל	נמם
מום	היי	יבמ	ראה	חבו	איע	מנק	דמב

In the last few years, a few books that speak about this ancient weapon surreptitiously muscled their way into the marketplace. I did my utmost to stop it from happening. But somehow, they pulled it off. I cannot mess with these letters. In fact, I am having a hard time right now even seeing them on the page.

This sequence of Aramaic is known as the 72 Names of God. They have the power to bypass me and reach the Divine instantly. But let me give you a heads-up: God does not answer prayers. God does not say *yes*. God does not say *no*. God just is.

What these letters will do is help you crash the Divine Realm so that you can use a few potent Forces of energy to help wipe me out. Now, before you're off and running, get this straight: The Divine Realm is not up in the sky. It's deep within the recesses of your consciousness. These letters reach deep inside you and extract me from your mind as quickly and as easily as a dentist extracts a baby tooth.

But you have to find me first. I am on the surface, but I am also deep within you. Here's a clue to spotting me: Ask your friends. That's right, ask your friends to describe your worst traits to you. Those traits are me. Now, use the force evoked by the 72 Names of God to connect to the energy and meditate to wipe me out. For good. But only if you dare. Only if you have the courage. Only if you can face the pain of losing your ego.

Meditate upon this ancient weapons system each day for five minutes. Focus your attention on eradicating my influences. Keep it simple. But keep it sincere. Do it with conviction.

PART IV:

THE FINAL CHAPTER

CHAPTER TWENTY:
THE VAULT

THE KEYS

When you pass a test, when you use the tools that God has handed you, you destroy me. The same holds true when you allow yourself to be uncomfortable, when you trust God, when you empathize with others, or wake up your yearning for your soul mate, or when you challenge your pain directly. You activate the keys that open up the vault that contains the infinite riches of the Energy of the Creator. The reason the world isn't swimming in a sea of bliss is because only a few have opened up the vault. But this has got to be a team effort. It takes more than a few brave souls to transform the world.

If you play nice, I'll reveal the greatest of all mysteries in regard to getting everything you want out of life.

THE VAULT, THE KEY, AND THE TIMER

There is a vault (not a bank vault—I am speaking metaphorically here). And this vault is on a timer. A very precise timer. Each time you insert the key into the lock, turn it, and open up the vault door, the timer is set. When the timer runs out, the vault slams shut. Getting the idea here? While that vault is open, you can grab as much as you want for yourself. But the only way to initially open the vault is by getting your hands on the key. The key, as I have told you, is the sharing you do when you pass the tests.

Now, here's where it gets a bit thorny. This key is magical. It knows what's inside your head. It knows what's inside your heart. None of us is perfect. Thus, none of us is able to pass every test.

Remember that my sole purpose is to make you fail—if not all the tests, at least the critical ones, those that set you up for real transformation. In order for me to fulfill my purpose, I remind you of your shame, your feelings of worthlessness, and the fact that you are a miserable failure. It's no wonder everyone hates tests. It's me working you from the inside, making you feel uncomfortable and worried that you're really nothing.

But if you understood this next critical idea, which we'll call the Ratio, I don't think you'd be so worried.

DETERMINING THE RATIO

What do I mean by the Ratio? Well, the Ratio determines how long the vault stays open. What determines the Ratio?

Your head—specifically your state of consciousness during a test. There is a direct correlation between the amount of growth that results from your actions and how long the vault stays open. Simple. Usually you are 100 percent in the status quo. Thus, the Ratio between where you were and where you have come is 100:1! Not only does that not open the vault, it doesn't even let you put your hands on the key. All you get is the swag I give away.

ALL THE SWAG

What do I mean by *swag*? Swag includes all the following: Comfort. Cars. Jewelry. Houses. Cash. Honor. Praise. Fame. Celebrity. Applause. Fake friends. Sex. Toys. Condos. Mistresses to put inside the condos. Prescription medications for your fears. Phobias and anxieties...

I think you catch my drift.

THE TREASURES

The treasures inside the Vault include the following: Growth. Happiness. Family. Love. Marriage. Children. Health. Well-being. Wisdom. Serenity. Peace of mind. Sustenance. A fearless, guiltless, anxiety-free life. True Friendship. Simple joy. Freedom. Appreciation. Bliss.

THE TRADE

Each time you accept swag, one of the real treasures in your life gets locked up in the vault. It's taken away from you. Poof! It's gone. Look again at the list of treasures. That's what you give up each time you make the swag your focus, or priority. And they stay locked in the vault until you make the swag your focus, or priority. choose the treasure. The good news is that you have many lifetimes to figure all this out, if you so choose.

This is why people lose their spouses, children, family, friends, financial security, careers, and their sanity. Because when the test comes, you lose your treasures in direct proportion to the amount of swag you choose at the time of the test. This means that losing a loved one, for instance, can occur in many ways. A divorce. A fight. Estrangement. Or death. The results are precisely calculated based on your decisions on the test.

So, this whole concept of punishment and reward—a nice God and a mean God—is totally bogus. You're the only one calling the shots here.

HOW GOD GIVES

God doesn't really answer your prayers. Big misconception propagated by yours truly. Rather, God is the answer to your prayers. Subtle difference. The word *is,* is a noun, not a verb.

What that means is that there is an Energy, a Force, a Power, that underlies all reality. This Power is God. And it's infinite. And it's filled with everything. This Power is hidden inside the vault. If you access it, it is the answer to your prayers.

THE PERCENTAGE GAME

When you go through a test and 20 percent of your action was genuinely unconditional, that means 80 percent of the act was influenced by a selfish, hidden agenda. Me.

But that's OK.

Seriously. It was still a positive action.

No need to worry because the treasure in the vault does not feed any selfish agenda. There's no swag in there, so the ego derives zip. It will only feed the unconditional aspect of your action.

Here's what happens: The key to the vault turns. The vault unlocks. The door opens wide. The timer on the door starts ticking. Your soul, your subconscious mind, and your conscious, willful desire start accumulating treasures from inside the vault. That door stays open in accordance with the 20 percent true growing that you did. Then the door gently closes.

Your life will now improve, relatively speaking, and become enriched with true fulfillment. This is the kind of fulfillment you tasted before, in the Garden of Eden. Honest. Believe me. It's transformative. Deeply loving. Eye-opening. You will wonder why you never sought this kind of fulfillment out before.

Actually, it was hidden away on purpose for reasons relating to free will. The fact is, your entire life, you were never whom you were meant to be. Not in the Divine sense, that is. You only took. Even when you performed positive actions, they were motivated by winning the approval of others. Or praise. Honor. A return favor. Your name on a building. A plaque. A tax break. Or just selfish pleasure. There's nothing wrong with pleasure. It's just that selfish pleasure doesn't last.

You are all creatures of comfort. Know why? Because that is your true origin and home—and it's your final destiny. Comfort and contentment are where you came from and they are where you will wind up, if you play your cards right. But in the short term, they're a roadblock. They stop you from walking into the vault.

So, the tests must be uncomfortable. They have to take you out of your comfort zone. No growth happens when you're sucking your thumb and holding on to your blanket. You have to hate the thought of what you are being challenged to do.

After you do it, you'll feel differently. But not one second before.

WHAT DO THE TESTS MEAN RIGHT NOW?

For today, a test might mean that for once you will learn to let go of your anger. It'll hurt. It'll be uncomfortable. After all, getting angry feels so satisfying. But when you hold your tongue, you're transforming yourself from a creature controlled by me to one controlled by your soul.

For today, passing a test might mean you do your job at the office for the sake of growing and becoming better, or for the sake of helping the company, and not out of a sense of obligation or fear. The paycheck you receive will be an automatic Effect of your actions.

Likewise, you pass a test by paying your employees good money because you want them to be the best they can be. You want them to feel good about themselves and all that they do, so that they, as well as your business, can thrive, and so that you can employ others and enrich their lives.

You become like God when you manufacture goods to enrich the lives of others, not to turn a profit. The profit will come, but it must be the Effect, not the Cause, of your work.

Catch the shift in consciousness here?

For 2000 years, you had your eye on the wrong ball. You did it all backwards. And you bled because of it.

I know. No one in their right mind thinks like this. Know why?

Because I have been everyone's "right mind" for thousands of years!

2000 YEARS OF RECEIVING

The entire world has been cast under a spell—one so powerful, it blinded you to the true reality. The spell is called *ego.* And the nature of ego is to receive. Every action throughout history, every single thought and flow of consciousness, was grounded in self-interest. And this is why you have not experienced a world of peace and unending miracles. I've got news for you. Chaos is *not* normal, and miracles are nature's true expressions. You just haven't figured out how to ignite those miracles yet. Well, now you know. The switch in consciousness is the method.

When you switch your consciousness from receiving and self-interest (me) into unconditional sharing and selfless behavior (God), you tap the real fulfillment of life.

Now comes the real mind-bending part.

THE FULFILLMENT EFFECT

The very fulfillment you draw from the vault has an additional benefit. It produces a secondary effect. The fulfillment that you feel will actually help further eradicate me. So, not only does it give you deep joy, it weakens me.

Now you're in the double bonus. The very joy you receive gently and seamlessly transforms your consciousness so that you can receive even more joy.

I am now telling you how to terminate my command with extreme prejudice. In your next test, work a little harder. This time, devote 35 percent on truly giving and growing. This keeps the vault open even longer so that you can grab even more eternal treasure. This Divine flow of fulfillment makes you happier than you ever thought possible, plus it negates even more of my power and influence over you. See what's happening?

You are growing happier as I grow weaker. Each test takes you closer to the ultimate—100 percent!

THE MAGIC

Knowing how to maximize your time in the vault requires that you completely grasp the idea of "Love Thy Neighbor as Thyself." For 2000 years, no one had a clue what this meant. It sounded nice. All warm and fuzzy. But it was just something to aspire to. But not any longer.

Most of the time, you put yourself first, right? When you think of others as you think of yourself, then you are putting others first, too. You are sharing with them as you share with yourself. This is greed, certainly, but it's greed turned upside down, and inside out.

It's greed turned into ultimate sharing. And how ironic that I would be the one to get you to understand what Moses, Jesus, and the Prophet Muhammad tried to tell you for so many centuries!

"Love Thy Neighbor as Thyself" is the master key to a luminous, Light-filled vault that has been hidden away since the world began! And it contains a never-ending flow of happiness, contentment, serenity, bountiful pleasure, deep peace of mind, and joyous laughter that you could never dream up in a million years!

Now, here comes the payoff—and it includes immortality.

Why? How?

Simple. The treasure inside the vault is made up of an infinite, endless, flow of Divine Energy. That means that when the vault remains eternally open, you nourish and draw Divine sustenance eternally. You keep sharing and God keeps giving...forever.

THE VAULT, THE SUN, AND THE SECOND LAW OF THERMODYNAMICS

The Second Law of Thermodynamics is a funny thing. Physicists say that over time, systems tend toward disorder, which is why things wear out and fall apart. What they do not realize is that this only happens because of the existence of space and time—two concepts created by me.

Here's how it works: I make you react and receive selfishly, and the energy involved slowly dissipates. However, when someone shares, energy is injected into the system. Instead of bringing about slow decay and death, it brings about life. When you tap the vault continuously, energy will flow continuously. Consequently, the tendency toward chaos described by the Second Law will be forever postponed. And the energy that flows into our world will forever sustain life and increase happiness and pleasure on this sacred planet.

NO FAVORS

By now, it should be clear: You are not doing the other person any favors when you love them unconditionally. That's the paradox. You're doing yourself a favor. The ultimate favor. You're practicing the most unselfish kind of greed there is—greed for the Light of the Creator by way of banishing the ego. You choose true fulfillment through sharing instead of selecting foolish selfishness in return for a bit of swag from *Satan*.

FREE GIFT WITH PURCHASE

Consider this next bit a free gift with purchase of this book.

Here's your gift: A few priceless suggestions to do with what you will. First off, thank your Uncle Satan for outing himself after a few millennia of ingenious concealment. Next, give a tip of the hat to God for creating you and allowing you to finally seize hold of this knowledge. In fact, do that right now. Take a moment and thank both of us for giving you the opportunity to exist and earn the miracles coming your way.

CHAPTER TWENTY ONE:

HAPPY ENDINGS

The greatest stories are those with happy endings. No one really likes an unhappy or scary ending. God doesn't. Even I don't. And I am sure you don't, either—especially when the story is the story of your own life. Therefore, you'll be glad to know that the greatest story ever told (the gem of a book you're reading right now) arrives at a happy, cornball ending, too. Formulaic, yes. But this is God's formula; I can't rewrite it.

No doom and gloom, no monsters from outer space, fireballs, or flesh-eating viruses. Sure, that stuff makes for great movies, and I have enjoyed (immensely) perpetuating those apocalyptic tales. But all fun aside, there is a deeper reason behind why I projected those images into your head. It was so that you could reject the doom and gloom, rise above it, and reach for happiness instead. Over the centuries, you suffered, but you were only spiraling toward disaster because you lacked the knowledge that I've revealed in this book.

But now you know everything. No more excuses. Forever starts now. The world has blamed *Satan* for all the evil in the world for centuries. No more. It's over. Put away the gun. Dismantle the dirty bomb. And get out from underneath the covers.

Your world is waiting for you to create it.

Oh, before I go, there's one last thing...

CHAPTER TWENTY TWO:

MY BIG ANNOUNCEMENT

A true autobiography is written when a person's life and career is at an end—unlike celebrities who write their memoirs in their 30s and 40s. How arrogant and pretentious, right? As you know, I've been at this Game now for more than 5000 years. I'm exhausted. Plus, I know that I'm destined to lose in the end, so why drag this genocide, pain, and suffering on any longer?

Let's cut to the chase, shall we? Hold on to your hats, kids.

I'm retiring.

It all makes sense now, doesn't it? The potentially damaging revelations. The candor. Yes, I'm hanging up my hat. I'm ready for my farewell party and my pension plan. After all, I did my job. I did it well. Almost too well. And now I'm done. Finito. Adiós. So long, suckers. It's been real.

I am not going to drop a meteor on you as I walk out. Or coax you into firing a nuclear weapon. Or scare the bejesus out of you. Now that I've revealed the Rules of the Game and my true purpose, all that can come to an end. Everyone will simply read my book and spread the good word with exponential speed. And you will choose, on your own, to create and enter a new miraculous and loving world, seamlessly, effortlessly, and ridiculously joyfully.

EPILOGUE:

A Final Confession

Psst! Come a little closer. I've got a secret for you.

You want to know how I got my job?

> *Yes, I'm just a soul whose intentions are good*
> *Oh Lord, please don't let me be misunderstood.*
> —The Animals

Sorry, I couldn't help myself. I am not a soul; I am an angel and, despite appearances, my intentions have always been good. They still are. So, what's a nice angel like me doing in a God-forsaken place like this?

I ate from the apple first!

Yep, before Adam and Eve took their bite, I took mine. That's why God gave me the job of helping you overcome your shame after Adam and Eve went down that same road. For one thing, I knew their shame all too well. For another, by helping you, I was helping myself. Funny how those Universal Laws work for everyone, even me! And now, with a little help from you, I can enjoy the world as it was always intended to be.

Thanks for hearing me out, and enjoy!

About the Centres

Below is a statement written by Rav Berg in 1984. It remains true today.

Through the ultimate knowledge and mystical practices of Kabbalah, one can reach the highest spiritual levels attainable. Although many people rely on belief, faith, and dogmas in pursuing the meaning of life, Kabbalists seek a spiritual connection with the Creator and the forces of the Creator, so that the strange becomes familiar, and faith becomes knowledge.

Throughout history, those who knew and practiced the Kabbalah were extremely careful in their dissemination of the knowledge because they knew the masses of mankind had not yet prepared for the ultimate truth of existence. Today, kabbalists know that it is not only proper but necessary to make the Kabbalah available to all who seek it.

The Kabbalah Centre is an independent, non-profit institute founded in Israel in 1922. The Centre provides research, information, and assistance to those who seek the insights of Kabbalah. The Centre offers public lectures, classes, seminars, and excursions to mystical sites at branches in Israel and in the United States. Branches have been opened in Mexico, Montreal, Toronto, Paris, Hong Kong, and Taiwan.

Our courses and materials deal with the Zoharic understanding of each weekly portion of the Torah. Every facet of life is covered and other dimensions, hithertofore unknown, provide a deeper connection to a superior reality. Three important beginner courses cover such aspects as: Time, Space and Motion; Reincarnation, Marriage, Divorce; Kabbalistic Meditation; Limitation of the Five Senses; Illusion-Reality; Four Phases; Male and Female, Death, Sleep, Dreams; Food; and Shabbat.

Thousands of people have benefited from the Centre's activities, and the Centre's publishing of kabbalistic material continues to be the most comprehensive of its kind in the world, including translations in English, Hebrew, Russian, German, Portuguese, French, Spanish, Farsi (Persian). Kabbalah can provide one with the true meaning of their being and the knowledge necessary for their ultimate benefit. It can show one spirituality that is beyond belief. The Kabbalah Centre will continue to make available the Kabbalah to all those who seek it.

—Rav Berg, 1984

About The Zohar

The Zohar, the basic source of the Kabbalah, was authored two thousand years ago by Rabbi Shimon bar Yochai while hiding from the Romans in a cave in Peki'in for 13 years. It was later brought to light by Rabbi Moses de Leon in Spain, and further revealed through the Safed Kabbalists and the Lurianic system of Kabbalah.

The programs of The Kabbalah Centre have been established to provide opportunities for learning, teaching, research, and demonstration of specialized knowledge drawn from the ageless wisdom of the Zohar and the Jewish sages. Long kept from the masses, today this knowledge of the Zohar and Kabbalah should be shared by all who seek to understand the deeper meaning of this spiritual heritage, and a deeper and more profound meaning of life. Modern science is only beginning to discover what our sages veiled in symbolism. This knowledge is of a very practical nature and can be applied daily for the betterment of our lives and of humankind.

Darkness cannot prevail in the presence of Light. Even a darkened room must respond to the lighting of a candle. As we share this moment together we are beginning to witness, and indeed some of us are already participating in, a people's revolution of enlightenment. The darkened clouds of strife and conflict will make their presence felt only as long as the Eternal Light remains concealed.

The Zohar now remains an instrument to infuse the cosmos with the revealed Lightforce of the Creator. The Zohar is not a book about religion. Rather, the Zohar is concerned with the relationship between the unseen forces of the cosmos, the Lightforce, and the impact on humanity.

The Zohar promises that with the ushering in of the Age of Aquarius, the cosmos will become readily accessible to human understanding. It states that in the days of the Messiah "there will no longer be the necessity for one to request of his neighbor, teach me wisdom." (Zohar, Naso 9:65) "One day, they will no longer teach every man his neighbor and every man his brother, saying know the Lord. For they shall all know Me, from the youngest to the oldest of them. (Jeremiah 31:34) We can regain dominion of our lives and environment. To achieve this objective, the Zohar provides us with an opportunity to transcend the crushing weight of universal negativity.

The daily perusing of the Zohar, without any attempt at translation or understanding will fill our consciousness with the Light, improving our well-being, and influencing all in our environment toward positive attitudes. Even the scanning of the Zohar by those unfamiliar with the Hebrew Alef Bet will accomplish the same result.

The connection that we establish through scanning the Zohar is one of unity with the Light of the Creator. The letters, even if we do not consciously know Hebrew or Aramaic, are the channels through which the connection is made and can be likened to dialing a telephone number or typing in the codes to run a computer program. The connection is established at the metaphysical level of our being and radiates into our physical plane of existence. But first there is the prerequisite of metaphysical "fixing." We have to consciously, through positive thought and actions, permit the immense power of the Zohar to radiate love, harmony, and peace into our lives for us to share with all humanity and the universe.

As we enter the years ahead, the Zohar will continue to be a people's book, striking a sympathetic chord in the hearts and minds of those who long for peace, truth, and relief from suffering. In the face of crises and catastrophe, the Zohar has the ability to resolve agonizing human afflictions by restoring each individual's relationship with the Lightforce of the Creator.

—Rav Berg, 1984

Kabbalah Centre Books

72 Names of God, The: Technology for the Soul
72 Names of God for Kids, The: A Treasury of Timeless Wisdom
72 Names of God Meditation Book, The
And You Shall Choose Life: An Essay on Kabbalah, the Purpose of Life, and Our True Spiritual Work
AstrologiK: Kabbalistic Astrology Guide for Children
Becoming Like God: Kabbalah and Our Ultimate Destiny
Beloved of My Soul: Letters of Our Master and Teacher Rav Yehuda Tzvi Brandwein to His Beloved Student, Kabbalist Rav Berg
Consciousness and the Cosmos (Previously Star Connection)
Days of Connection: A Guide to Kabbalah's Holidays and New Moons
Days of Power Part 1
Days of Power Part 2
Education of a Kabbalist
Energy of the Hebrew Letters, The
Fear is Not an Option
Finding the Light Through the Darkness: Inspirational Lessons Rooted in the Bible and the Zohar
God Wears Lipstick: Kabbalah for Women
Holy Grail, The: A Manifesto on the Zohar
Immortality: The Inevitability of Eternal Life
Kabbalah Connection, The: Preparing the Soul for Pesach
Kabbalah for the Layman
Kabbalah Method, The: The Bridge Between Science and the Soul, Physics and Fulfillment, Quantum and the Creator
Kabbalah: The Power To Change Everything
Kabbalistic Astrology: And the Meaning of Our Lives
Kabbalistic Bible: Genesis
Kabbalistic Bible: Exodus
Kabbalistic Bible: Leviticus
Kabbalistic Bible: Numbers
Kabbalistic Bible: Deuteronomy

Light of Wisdom: On Wisdom, Life, and Eternity
Miracles, Mysteries, and Prayer Volume 1
Miracles, Mysteries, and Prayer Volume 2
Nano: Technology of Mind Over Matter
Navigating The Universe: A Roadmap for Understanding the Cosmic Influences that Shape Our Lives (Previously Time Zones)
On World Peace: Two Essays by the Holy Kabbalist Rav Yehuda Ashlag
Path to the Light: Decoding the Bible with Kabbalah: Book of Beresheet Volume 1
Path to the Light: Decoding the Bible with Kabbalah: Book of Beresheet Volume 2
Path to the Light: Decoding the Bible with Kabbalah: Book of Beresheet Volume 3
Path to the Light: Decoding the Bible with Kabbalah: Book of Beresheet Volume 4
Path to the Light: Decoding the Bible with Kabbalah: Book of Shemot Volume 5
Path to the Light: Decoding the Bible with Kabbalah: Book of Shemot Volume 6
Path to the Light: Decoding the Bible with Kabbalah: Book of Vayikra Volume 7
Path to the Light: Decoding the Bible with Kabbalah: Book of Bamdibar Volume 8
Path to the Light: Decoding the Bible with Kabbalah: Book of Bamdibar Volume 9
Power of Kabbalah, The: 13 Principles to Overcome Challenges and Achieve Fulfillment
Rethink Love: 3 Steps to Being the One, Attracting the One, and Becoming One
Satan: An Autobiography
Secret, The: Unlocking the Source of Joy & Fulfillment
Secrets of the Bible: Teachings from Kabbalistic Masters
Secrets of The Zohar: Stories and Meditations to Awaken the Heart
Simple Light: Wisdom from a Woman's Heart
Shabbat Connections

Taming Chaos: Harnessing the Secret Codes of the Universe to Make Sense of Our Lives

Thought of Creation, The: On the Individual, Humanity, and Their Ultimate Perfection

To Be Continued: Reincarnation & the Purpose of Our Lives

To the Power of One

True Prosperity: How to Have Everything

Two Unlikely People to Change the World: A Memoir by Karen Berg

Vokabbalahry: Words of Wisdom for Kids to Live By

Way of the Kabbalist, The: A User's Guide To Technology for the Soul

Well of Life: Kabbalistic Wisdom from a Depth of Knowledge

Wheels of the Soul: Kabbalah and Reincarnation

Wisdom of Truth, The: 12 Essays by the Holy Kabbalistn Rav Yehuda Ashlag

Zohar, The

Rav Berg was born August 20, 1927, in New York City. After many years of traditional religious study, he was ordained as a rabbi at Torah VaDaat. A businessman who wanted to make a difference in this world, he was always searching for his true path. Upon a chance meeting with Rav Yehuda Brandwein, Rav Berg knew he had found his teacher, and moved to Israel to study with Rav Brandwein at The Kabbalah Centre. After he returned to New York, Rav Berg maintained a written correspondence with Rav Brandwein who passed on his legacy as Director of The Kabbalah Centre to Rav Berg.

Rav Berg made it his mission to continue editing, writing, printing, and distributing all that he learned from his teacher and began sharing the secrets of Kabbalah texts, which historically had been reserved for scholars. His book, Kabbalah for the Layman, was the revolutionary step that made Kabbalah accessible to every person. Rav Berg's other books include The Kabbalah Connection, Wheels of a Soul: Kabbalah and Reincarnation, To the Power of One, Energy of the Hebrew Letters, Immortality, Nano, The Kabbalah Method, Taming Chaos, and Education of a Kabbalist.

Together with his wife, Karen, Rav Berg opened the doors of The Kabbalah Centre to all who desire to learn this universal wisdom. Rav Berg left the world in September 2013, and Karen Berg departed in July 2020. Following their passing, their son Michael Berg continues their vision and their work as the Director of The Kabbalah Centre.

www.ingramcontent.com/pod-product-compliance
Lightning Source LLC
LaVergne TN
LVHW052336100826
845147LV00020B/1079

* 9 7 8 1 5 7 1 8 9 9 9 6 5 *